Proto
An Undergraduate Humanities Journal

Volume 1
2010
Eyewitness

Proto
An Undergraduate Humanities Journal
Volume 1
2010
Eyewitness

Editors
Jean Lee Cole
Alex Hooke

Apprentice House
Baltimore, Maryland

Copyright © 2011 Loyola University Maryland

All rights reserved. No part of this book may be reproduced or transmitted in any form or by any means, electronic or mechanical, including photocopy, recording, or any information storage and retrieval system, without prior permission from the publisher (except by reviewers who may quote brief passages).

This publication was supported with grants from Stevenson University and the Loyola University Maryland Center for the Humanities.

ISBN: 978-1-934074-66-4

Printed in the United States of America

First Edition

Published by Apprentice House
The Future of Publishing...Today!

Apprentice House
Communication Department
Loyola University Maryland
4501 N. Charles Street
Baltimore, MD 21210

410.617.5265
410.617.2198 (fax)
www.ApprenticeHouse.com
info@ApprenticeHouse.com

Editorial Board

Jane Bennett
Professor of Political Science
The Johns Hopkins University

Jean Lee Cole
Associate Professor of English
Loyola University Maryland

Alex Hooke
Professor of Philosophy
Stevenson University

Flo Martin
Professor of French
Goucher College

Helen Mitchell
Professor of Philosophy
Howard County Community College

Reanna Ursin
Assistant Professor of English
McDaniel College

Jennifer Ballengee
Associate Professor of English
Towson University

Susanna Throop
Assistant Professor of History
Ursinus College

Proto: An Undergraduate Humanities Journal
Volume 1, 2010

ix   Editor's Note

1   Eyewitness: Papers from the 2010 Stevenson University Undergraduate Conference

     3   From Humbug to Lovebug: Scrooge's Transformations in *A Christmas Carol*
         Rachel Lyons, Stevenson University

     17   Beauty Witness
         Jobie Watson, Howard Community College

     21   Shattered: Collapse of the Twin Towers
         Tom Pisciotta, Chesapeake College

35   Open Submissions

     37   Middle-Text: Orality and Literacy in *Middlesex*
         Melissa Pankake, Ursinus College

     48   Suffering and the Happiness Movement: What Would Nietzsche Do?
         Daniel Murphy, Towson University

     64   Hopkins Goes To War
         Fletcher Boone, The Johns Hopkins University

     85   Shaving With the Grain: Portraying an Effective Iago
         Tony Levero, Loyola University Maryland

     95   Reviewing the Various Stages of Shakespeare's *Macbeth*
         Jennifer L. Bryant, Frostburg State University

     100   Who Needs the External World Anyway? Analyzing the Computational Theory and Methodological Solipsism
         Stephanie Amalfe, The Johns Hopkins University

107   Submission Guidelines

Editors' Note

Welcome to the inaugural issue of *Proto,* an annual, humanities-centered journal that will disseminate undergraduate scholarship from institutions in the mid-Atlantic region. The journal's title expresses its ethos. According to the Oxford English Dictionary, the prefix *proto-* connotes something that is the "earliest, original; at an early stage of development, primitive; incipient, potential." At its best, undergraduate scholarship embodies all of these qualities. While it almost certainly constitutes scholarship at an early stage of development, it also has the potential to be original and innovative; the seeds of future thought often take root during the undergraduate years. We see this journal as a site for this process of germination and growth.

By restricting the journal's geographic range to the mid-Atlantic region, we hope to provide opportunities for intellectual exchange between area institutions, not only at the undergraduate level, but among faculty as well. The idea of a journal grew out of the success of the Stevenson University Undergraduate Conference in Baltimore, Maryland, which brings together participants from colleges in Maryland, Virginia, Pennsylvania, and Delaware. This conference, which has been held every spring since 2001, is an excellent opportunity for undergraduates to present their work to peers from other institutions. It also has fostered intercampus connections between faculty who have sponsored students for the conference. Each issue of *Proto* will feature a selection of the best essays from the conference; the 2010 conference theme was "Eyewitness," which the three authors included here have adapted to their particular subjects.

Proto also includes a selection of essays submitted by individual students and reviewed by a board of faculty members from a variety of colleges and universities in the mid-Atlantic region. Guidelines for submitting essays are included at the end of the issue.

We hope you are inspired by the creativity and intellect of the scholars' work included here. Please pass on word of *Proto* to friends and colleagues!

Jean Lee Cole
Department of English
Loyola University Maryland

Alex Hooke
Department of Philosophy
Stevenson University

Papers from the 2010 Stevenson University Undergraduate Conference

Theme: Eyewitness

From Humbug to Lovebug: Scrooge's Transformations in *A Christmas Carol*

Rachel Lyons
Stevenson University

Introduction

If we are born knowing ourselves, our purpose and how to fulfill it, and how we die, life appears very predictable and dull. Our capabilities and capacities grow and become more known to us through firsthand experience. Ebenezer Scrooge in Charles Dickens' *A Christmas Carol* does not "know [him]self" and lives "the unexamined life" that Socrates would deem "not worth living" because he does not yet understand how important his life is to others around him (Plato 44, 66). On a fateful Christmas Eve night, Scrooge crumbles, broken in spirit, and transforms into an emotional human being who holds the capability to amend his ways and possesses the capacity to love his fellow man.

Vincent Newey suggests that the conflict between self-deception and self-knowledge creates "an individual who lives to struggle and struggles to live" (28). Such a man is Ebenezer Scrooge, whose external reality is an isolated world focused entirely on his business. Everything that does not involve his work is irrelevant and regarded as an interruption. He speaks only in terms of business and money, so he lacks any friendly social communication with his nephew and his clerk. Through the visitation of the Spirits, Scrooge's internal deficiencies

Rachel Lyons recently graduated from Stevenson University as a Film/Video/Theatre major, with a concentration in Theatre and a minor in English. She is working part-time in theatre and plans on going to graduate school for Scenic Design or Dramaturgy. When not involved in theatre, she crochets and writes poetry.

come to light. He faces his Past, Present, and Future and rediscovers who he really is. These epiphanies effectively transform him into a new being who "knows" himself. Since Dickens concentrates his focus on Scrooge's actions, not his thoughts, film actors have artistic freedom to interpret Scrooge's inner turmoil. The film adaptations of the *Carol* that I have chosen for this paper offer alterations of the original story, including added scenes or dialogue to enhance and increase the story's dramatic action.

The Christmas Eve night of self-reflection costs Ebenezer Scrooge his life motto—"Bah, humbug"—his cold and unfeeling shell, even his self-deceptions and vices. When he faces his Past, the Present, and his current Future, he experiences nostalgia and emotions that he has never felt or known before. As these new sensations eventually reshape his life and increase his self-knowledge, he begins to maintain stronger relationships with his nephew Fred, his clerk Bob Cratchit, and his clients. What he learns about himself in one night requires a lifetime of learning for anyone seeking to lead an examined life.

"Christmas? Bah, humbug!": Who Is Scrooge?

> Oh! but he was a tight-fisted hand at the grindstone, Scrooge, a squeezing, wrenching, grasping, scraping, clutching, covetous, old sinner! Hard and sharp as flint, from which no steel had ever struck out generous fire; secret and self-contained.... He carried his own low temperature always about with him... (Dickens 4)

This description presents the classic and stereotypical miser that is Ebenezer Scrooge. He is a confident man, with no apparent fears of anything going wrong... or so it seems. On this particular Christmas Eve, Scrooge experiences the usual disruptions and irritations to his business day: his nephew visits, gentlemen are seeking donations for a charitable cause, and his clerk wants Christmas Day off. Scrooge's robotic and routine patterns are defenses that keep him from having to deal with "human sympathy" as he "edge[s] his way along the crowded paths of life" (Dickens 4). Dickens doesn't make specific the nature of the business "Scrooge and Marley," beyond the suggestion that it is a counting-house. One possibility may be that the company engages in the practice of usury, in which "money and the profits born from money, not labor" are placed on a pedestal above friendship, love, and the liberations of body and soul (Kleinberg 98). This lack of specificity about the business permits film adaptations to speculate about the nature and scope of Scrooge's power over his clients. For example, in the 1970 musical *Scrooge*, starring Albert Finney, his clients work in the marketplace and pay their dues on Christmas Eve. When they do not have the money they owe to Scrooge, he reluctantly allows them more time but increases their debt.

"Bah, humbug" represents Scrooge's personal and business motto. It captures his lack of trust in a person's words or intent until they are proven to his satisfaction. Though Bob Cratchit must have proven himself trustworthy enough to be Scrooge's clerk, the pressure of the business is relentless and keeps Scrooge suspicious (Dickens 8). Bob Cratchit and Scrooge's nephew Fred represent Scrooge's alter egos: they are both full of the Christmas spirit—happy, "warmer than Scrooge" (Dickens 7), and poor. Fred's belief that Christmas is a time when even the hardest of hearts can freely open to others and treat them as equals (Dickens 6) will ultimately be vindicated. However, the "Bah, humbug" attitude of their employer makes one wonder how Fred and Bob Cratchit can even think of having a merry Christmas?

Some portly gentlemen seek a donation from Scrooge to help the poor and destitute at this especially difficult time of the year, "when Want is keenly felt, and Abundance rejoices" (Dickens 8). Even though he has the money to make a generous donation, Scrooge chooses to remain miserly, stating that the union workhouses will provide for them (Dickens 8). In the events that will unfold this Christmas Eve, Scrooge's words will return to accuse him. At the close of business, however, it seems to him just another ordinary and melancholic day at work...until he goes home for the night.

The Knocker and Visitation

This Christmas marks seven years since the passing of Scrooge's business partner, Jacob Marley. Dickens notes that "Scrooge had not bestowed one thought on Marley, since his last mention of his seven years' dead partner that afternoon" (Dickens 10). However, when Scrooge arrives home, Marley's face appears on his door knocker. It stops Scrooge and startles him out of his robotic routine. In many of the film adaptations, Marley's face calls out to Scrooge from the knocker. However, in the musical *Scrooge* (1970) and the newly-released Disney version *A Christmas Carol* (2009), Scrooge attempts to touch the knocker to test its reality. In *Scrooge*, Marley's face disappears before Scrooge's hand reaches it (1970). In the Disney film, Marley's face appears with his eyes and mouth shut. The camera cuts back and forth between Scrooge and the knocker to create the wonder and suspense of the phenomenon. Before Scrooge's hand can touch Marley's face, it suddenly opens its eyes and mouth with a gasp, making Scrooge suddenly start back, slip on the ice, fall backward down his front steps (and without losing his hat!), take cover, and peek up to the now-normal knocker from the top step. (*A Christmas Carol* 2009)

Disturbed by seeing his former partner's face on his knocker, Scrooge double locks himself in and attempts to settle in for the night, checking for anything suspicious. Then, Marley's face appears on the fireplace tiles, the bells sound involuntarily, the cellar-door suddenly flings open, and the sound of chains clanking rises up the steps (Dickens 12-13). Scrooge attempts to dismiss these happenings as "humbug," but he grows more and more uncertain and uneasy. When Marley's ghost walks into the room, his countenance falls and the candle goes out on its own (Dickens 13). Attempting to "keep down his terror" (Dickens 14), Scrooge "tremble[s]" (15), and "quakes exceedingly" (16). He attempts to keep a distance between himself and the ghost. He does so successfully in the musical *Scrooge* (1970) and in *A Christmas Carol* (1984) with George C. Scott. In Disney's recent film, however, Scrooge remains cowering in his fireside chair when Marley in chains come face-to-face with him (*A Christmas Carol* 2009). His feeble attempt to rationalize Marley's appearance as a hallucination resulting from his undigested dinner (Dickens 14) fails miserably, as Scrooge falls to his knees begging for mercy (15) and begins questioning the ghost.

"Marley is, in fact, like a double to Scrooge, a deceased double… this is where the boundary begins to blur between the external setting and the inner world of Ebenezer Scrooge" (Eirik 83). Scrooge easily identifies with Marley because they were business partners and had similar views of the world. Now, as Marley agonizes about his life of missed opportunities and his afterlife without rest or peace (Dickens 15-16). Scrooge appears confused; after all, Marley was a good man of business. Marley's chilling response is:

> Business! … Mankind was my business. The common welfare was my business; charity, mercy, forbearance, and benevolence, were,

all, my business. The dealings of my trade were but a drop of water in the comprehensive ocean of my business! (Dickens 16)

Marley has supplied the missing link between Scrooge and humanity that Fred had asserted at the office. In a series of Spirit visitations, Scrooge will be given a second chance. As Marley's ghost departs, a shaken Scrooge tries to dismiss even this as humbug, "but stop[s] at the first syllable" (Dickens 18); this is the last time he uses his motto.

Past: Forgotten Hopes and Joys

André Comte-Sponville defines courage as "the capacity to overcome fear" (44) and fear as "a necessary and sufficient element of courage" (51); therefore, a person cannot have courage without first having fear. When the Spirits visit, Scrooge enters "an alternate, invisible world where time, gravity, and matter itself are subject to different laws" (Epstein 178-179). Stephen Bertman compares Scrooge's journey to Dante's in the *Inferno*. Both protagonists have guides (Virgil for Dante and the Spirits for Scrooge) to show how their lives are flawed. While Satan is eternally damned, Scrooge's soul, "thanks to Dickens... could qualify for salvation" (Bertman 169). Through the guidance of the Spirit of Christmas Past, Scrooge sees how he became the business man he is through visions of ignored loved ones and missed opportunities.

As Scrooge participates in the celebrations and important events of his past life, he becomes self-conscious when he notices the Spirit looking on. Still, he recollects "a thousand odours floating in the air, each one connected with a thousand thoughts, and hopes, and joys, and cares long, long, forgotten" (Dickens 22). He weeps remembering how lonely the Christmas holiday was for him being separated from his friends and family.

One Christmas, his younger sister Fan comes to take him home, promising that their father has become kinder (Dickens 25). Dickens does not describe Scrooge's relationship with his parents, but one film establishes that Scrooge's mother died giving birth to him, and his living father holds him responsible for her death (*A Christmas Carol* 1984). Though Dickens does not describe Fan's death, a 1951 film version with Alastair Sim shows Scrooge promising his dying sister that he would do anything for her but leaving her bedside before hearing her final request. As the older Scrooge continues looking on, he hears for the first time her final request to take care of her son Fred. The Spirit tells Scrooge, "You heard her," and he weeps and begs her forgiveness. (*A Christmas Carol* 1951) Through Fan, Scrooge knows love and gains the capacity to love.

At Scrooge's former employer Fezziwig's annual Christmas party, Scrooge puts "his heart and soul in the scene," acting like "a man out of his wits." When he realizes the Spirit watching him, he "under[goes] the strangest agitation," as if he never wanted the party to end (Dickens 28-29). Scrooge remembers how happy he was: young, in love with a beautiful woman, and working for a wonderful and ideal employer. Fezziwig controls the finances (Dickens 29); yet once a year he spends money for a silly but fun and enjoyable party. Scrooge's own obsession with money prevents him from following Fezziwig's example. Now that he holds the same power, Scrooge stops to think about having a word with his clerk.

Belle is the first woman Scrooge has loved since his sister Fan's death. Though the next scene following the party shows Scrooge breaking up with Belle, many of the film adaptations show Scrooge dancing, conversing, and courting Belle (whose name changes in the films). They also show Scrooge foreshadowing his future with Belle: he becomes "proud and foolish" (*A Christmas Carol* 1951), thinking he will deserve her only when he makes his fortune (*A Christmas Carol* 1984). Of course, it is their love for each other that truly makes them happy.

The ever-beautiful Belle witnesses Scrooge's transformation into a wealthy business man. His new idol, money, replaces her, as his pursuit of the "the master-passion Gain" increases, his face shows signs of "care and avarice," and "an eager, greedy, restless motion in the eye" (Dickens 29). Belle releases him from his promise of marriage. An older Scrooge sadly looks on knowing that he chose gain and money through his business, over happiness and love with Belle. He realizes that a life of happiness is possible without security and money.

To this point in his elder years, Scrooge believes that he will never love anyone else the way he loved Fan and Belle. Though both his loves—Fan and Belle—are forever lost, their memories represent Scrooge's happier moments from his Past. These pleasant shadows help Scrooge see what others once saw in him: Fan saw a loving brother, Fezziwig a hard worker, and Belle a potential husband. His love and dedication were more appealing to others than large quantities of money. As visions of the past dissolve, the next Spirit will show

Scrooge what others perceive him to be in the present world and how his decisions affect the Christmas celebrations in his clerk's and nephew's households.

Present: Himself Through Others

When the Spirit of Christmas Present visits, Scrooge admits that he is currently processing a lesson from the former Spirit's visitation and wants to profit from whatever lesson the Spirit has to offer him (Dickens 36). In the films, however, Scrooge still shows a hardness of heart to change. He attempts to argue that he is too old to change (*A Christmas Carol* 1951) and that he hates life because life hates him (*Scrooge* 1970). The Spirit obligingly shows Scrooge that he unknowingly gives others more happiness than he thinks he does.

At their humble abode, Bob Cratchit, his wife, their youngest son Tiny Tim, and the other children come together to celebrate Christmas amid quaint surroundings and their small feast. Bob offers a toast to his employer as "the Founder of the Feast," knowing that if Scrooge did not employ him his family might be in worse conditions than they are now. Mrs. Cratchit is more of a realist, calling Scrooge "odious, stingy, hard, unfeeling" (Dickens 43). Though the Cratchits are poor, they are still "happy, grateful, and pleased with one another, and contented with time" (Dickens 44). They appreciate what they have.

Despite his disability, Tiny Tim is happy, within a family he loves. Wise for his young age, he offers a Christmas invocation, "God bless us everyone!" (Dickens 42). Scrooge connects through Tiny Tim with the childhood that he never knew and begins to feel for the child "an interest he had never felt before" (Dickens 43). When Scrooge begs the Spirit to spare Tiny Tim from death, the Spirit turns his own words against him, pointing out that the world's population would decrease with his death and proclaiming, "It may be, that in the sight of Heaven, you are more worthless and less fit to live than millions like this poor man's child" (Dickens 43). Scrooge "[hangs] his head," is overcome with "penitence and grief," and trembles with downcast eyes. These thoughts will return in the Future to haunt him.

Fred toasts his uncle for the happiness he has given to him and his wife. He has patience, pity, and compassion for his uncle and invites him every year for Christmas dinner, hoping that he will have a change of heart. Fred also hopes that his uncle will see the goodness in other people's hearts, regardless of how rich or poor they are (Dickens 47-50).

Before the aging Spirit leaves, a last vision horrifies Scrooge: the boy Ignorance and the girl Want. Their physicality as "yellow, meagre, ragged, scowling, wolfish" (Dickens 51-52) rebukes those who do not know of their existence and prefigures their downfall. Ignorance has "doom" written upon his brow while Want signifies greed, pride, and selfishness. Scrooge's newly awakened compassion for Tiny Tim leads him to inquire about a refuge or resource for the children Ignorance and Want. Calling up Scrooge's own words, the Spirit mockingly asks about the purpose of the prisons and workhouses (Dickens 52).

Newey describes the final test for redemption as "rich in colour" and the end of "a momentous process of transformation in which hard-won knowledge of self and others, and of their interdependence, brings ample return in enhancing both personal and collective existence" (18). The horrifying shadows of the final Spirit will challenge Scrooge to interpret the shadows for himself in a "realm beyond language" (Epstein 182) and see if his courage will stand even in the face of death.

Future: Profiting through Death

In Disney's *A Christmas Carol*, the Spirits' represent "forces from inside the old man's [Scrooge's] subconscious" (Anthony 2), so the Spirit of Christmas Future emanates from Scrooge's own shadow (2009). The Spirit of Christmas Yet to Come, like the previous Spirits, does not assume that Scrooge is ready for the change of heart. Scrooge is "filled with a solemn dread" and "fear[s] the silent shape so much that his legs trembled beneath him, and he found that he could hardly stand when he prepared to follow it" (Dickens 53). As he admits his fear, he understands that the Spirit's visitation is for his benefit and prepares to follow it (Dickens 54). As he struggles to apply what he has learned from the previous Spirits, Scrooge decides to "treasure up every word he heard, and everything he saw" (Dickens 55) because he wants to assure himself that his future will be happy and secure.

Oddly, Scrooge is absent from this vision of the Future. During the song "Thank You Very Much" in the 1970 musical, Scrooge joins the celebration without understanding that his debtors are thanking him for dying (*Scrooge* 1970). In the novella, the gentlemen at the Exchange do not mention the name of the man who died but wonder what will happen to his money and claim, "Old Scratch got his own at last" (Dickens 55). In a pawnshop in an obscure, foul part of town, Old Joe weighs the value of stolen items from a dead man's house brought in by a laundress, a charwoman, and an undertaker. This disrespect to the dead man is the same disrespect and greed that Scrooge had previously embraced. He is horrified knowing that this behavior reflects his own and seeks to change it (Dickens 59).

In the dark chamber from which the trio at Old Joe's had been stealing, Scrooge has a "secret impulse… to know what kind of room it was" (Dickens 59) because something seems eerily familiar to him, but his attention falls on the man lying dead underneath the bed sheet. The Spirit wants him to reveal who the dead man is, but Scrooge does not have the courage to do so. When Scrooge asks who feels for this man's death, the Spirit shows a couple grateful because they have more time to pay off their debt (Dickens 61). When Scrooge insists on seeing tenderness connected with death, Spirit leads them back to Bob Cratchit's home.

Recalling the previous Spirit's prediction, Scrooge knows that Tiny Tim has died and now understands that improving the child's health must be his first matter of business in trying to help his clerk's struggling family. In the Disney film, Scrooge weeps while sitting on the staircase leading up to the room where Tiny Tim was laid. When Bob Cratchit goes up to sit by his child, he pauses a moment on the step and comes unknowingly face-to-face with Scrooge. Scrooge sees the deep sadness in his employee's eyes and face and manages to choke out his name, trying to comfort him (*A Christmas Carol* 2009). In the 1984 film, Scrooge believes that this is the final shadow and asks the Spirit to take him home, but the Spirit directs him to a graveyard, the home of his future self.

Scrooge: The Dead Man

The graveyard scene brings the events of the night to fruition. As Scrooge faces the final test of his courage in the face of death, his ultimate fate, he assumes that his future self has profited from the Spirits' visitations and is out doing good deeds in the world. He does not want to believe that this dead man is himself, and questions the finality of the shadows (Dickens 65). The shadows that "Will be" secure Scrooge's fate as identical to that of his dead partner Marley and unchangeable, whereas the shadows that "May be" assure Scrooge that he still has time to change his ways. Scrooge indicates his understanding by observing, "Men's courses will foreshadow certain ends, to which, if persevered in, they must lead... But if the courses be departed from, the ends will change" (Dickens 65). It is his last thought before the name on the gravestone is revealed.

Film adaptations of the *Carol* vary the revelation of the name on the gravestone for dramatic effect. Some of the older traditional adaptations have Scrooge seeing or revealing his own name (1938; 1951; 1970; 1984). The musical *Scrooge* shows Scrooge suffering the consequences of his refusal to change... in Hell. Jacob Marley (Sir Alec Guinness) leads Scrooge (Albert Finney) from the hot depths of Hell to a freezing cold office where minions arrive and wrap Scrooge in his ponderous chain. (*Scrooge* 1970) Disney's three adaptations of the story take a different approach. *Mickey's Christmas Carol* shows the Spirit (played by Pete) striking a match against the gravestone and shining the light on it (1983). For *The Muppet Christmas Carol*, director Brian Henson notes that Michael Caine, playing Scrooge, knows that when the Spirit points to the gravestone the name on it is his own; he will do anything to keep from revealing his name (Henson 1993). Finally, in Disney's recent adaptation, the wind from the thundersnow blows the snow away, revealing Scrooge's name, the month, date, and year of birth, and the month and day of death. (*A Christmas Carol* 2009). Ultimately, Scrooge reaches the final and most difficult moment in his transformation.

The heart of the *Carol* is Scrooge reading his own name on the gravestone and suddenly realizing that his current life amounts to essentially nothing. He is the man laid out upon the bed, now revealed as less worthy of Heaven than Tiny Tim (Dickens 65, 43). He falls on his knees admitting to "a fate worse than death—a worthless life, without meaning except as a byword for unnaturalness, which is to be less than nothing" (Newey 39). This is the very definition of Socrates' "unexamined life" and a fear of the life he already lives: a life of isolation and without love. It is the charge that Bertman makes when he notes that Dante would send Scrooge to the Fourth Circle, where the miserly "[push] heavy weights that symboliz[e] the burden of materialism" (168). This final shadow of the Future forces Scrooge to make "a single choice of a worthy life and a life worth living: to participate in the social existence laid out for him, to which he has been at worst antagonistic and at best peripheral" (Newey 39). He vows to honor Christmas, live in the Past, Present, and Future, and prays in agony for the Spirit to let him have this chance at a life of redemption (Dickens 65).

Merry Christmas!: Spreading the Love

The scene transforms from the graveyard to the bedroom as an act of forgiveness of Scrooge for all the years of wasted opportunities, and pity for him because he "had been sobbing violently in his conflict with the Spirit" (Dickens 67). As the Spirit of Christmas Future allows Scrooge a second chance to live his life, a life of self-redemption, he awakes overjoyed to be alive and knowing that it is Christmas Day (Dickens 68). True, Scrooge cannot reverse decisions he has made in his distant past, but he can reverse decisions he made the day before, on Christmas Eve, and he begins the new day by sending the prize turkey to the Cratchits' home anonymously.

Instead of walking along the edge of the sidewalk, Scrooge now walks in the open, wishing everyone a merry Christmas. The flint finally strikes a generous fire, the secret of his great capacity for happiness reveals itself, and his low temperature has risen to friendly warmth. He finally finds a true happiness outside of his business. When he meets up with one of the portly gentlemen from the previous day, Scrooge asks for the gentleman's pardon, and gives his donation for their cause. The gentleman asks if he is serious, graciously accepts it, and agrees to visit the newly-generous Scrooge sometime (Dickens 70).

Despite his new attitude, Scrooge fears the reaction of his nephew Fred's family. He knows he has not been a part of his nephew's life and is not proud of his behavior towards him. "He passed the door [to Fred's house] a dozen times, before he had the courage to go up and knock. But he made a dash, and did it" (Dickens 70). When Scrooge shows up for Christmas dinner, Fred's hope for his uncle's change of heart comes true. Scrooge seeks forgiveness from his nephew, who mercifully allows his uncle in. The film adaptations show Scrooge modestly and quietly going into the room so as not to disturb the celebration or make a grand entrance. He knows that one day Fred will ask him what made him change his heart and mind. In the newest Disney film, Scrooge hears the Yes and No game from the shadow with the Spirit of Christmas Present: "Is it an ass?" "Yes ... and no." Sadly, he knows that both responses are true. "I've come to dinner..." he says, "if you'll have me," and everyone is overjoyed to see him (*A Christmas Carol* 2009). After being well received by all on Christmas

Day, Scrooge now needs to prove that his change of heart is permanent, which is why the *Carol* continues to the day after Christmas.

Comte-Sponville defines humor as "the virtue that can make us laugh at anything provided that we first laugh at ourselves… without hatred" (216). Bob Cratchit is the beneficiary, as Scrooge makes fun of his former self and how irrationally he was living his life. He acts as his former self and then says something that is quite unlike his former self (Dickens 71), which is raising his clerk's salary. The *Carol* ends with a final and positive look at the new Ebenezer Scrooge:

> Scrooge was better than his word. He did it all, and infinitely more; and to Tiny Tim, who did not die, he was a second father. He became as good a friend, as good a master, and as good a man, as the good old city, town, or borough, in the good old world. Some people laughed to see the alteration in him, but he let them laugh, and little heeded them… His own heart laughed: and that was quite enough for him. (Dickens 72)

Scrooge transforms from the melancholic misanthrope to one of London's best and well-known citizens. He is an even more excellent man of business, a better employer and friend to his clerk and his family, and a loving uncle to his nephew. "[T]he real ending is not even an ending: it is a happy beginning" (Eirik 88), as Ebenezer Scrooge returns to society embracing "charity, mercy, benevolence, and forbearance" (Dickens 16), emotions, and true self-knowledge.

Conclusion: Humbug to Lovebug

Throughout *A Christmas Carol*, Scrooge transforms from a Humbug to the Lovebug. For the purpose of this paper, the noun "humbug" represents a person living in the midst of self-deceptions. Newey suggests, "We are never more in chains perhaps than when we think ourselves free" (19). Scrooge believes that life is fine, but his isolation keeps him from fulfilling social obligations and enjoying human relationships. The ghost of Jacob Marley shocks Scrooge out of this barren routine. In recollecting his Past, Scrooge feels sadness and regret for a lost childhood, but loses his sense of self and rejoins what was once happiness for him. Through the Present, Scrooge recognizes that even among the worst and poorest conditions, the most pitiful people still have a merry Christmas because they appreciate what they have. Finally, the Spirit of Christmas Future subjects Scrooge to the life that others around him will know once he is dead and gone. Ironically, his only connection to the Future is through the man lying dead on the bed. Every person in the Future represents a part of Scrooge, the Humbug, which now horrifies him. Seeing his own grave is like looking at himself in a mirror as he was before the self-reflective journey. Now that he knows himself, Scrooge vows never to be like that again.

Finally, Christmas Day arrives and the Humbug becomes a Lovebug, a person who spreads love and joy, or in Scrooge's case, the "charity, mercy, forbearance, and benevolence" that Marley spoke of as a part of the business of mankind. Scrooge's acts of kindness on Christmas Day begin his new journey of seeking forgiveness from others and transforming his life into an examined life that is very much worth living.

Works Cited

A Christmas Carol. Dir. Clive Donner. Perfs. George C. Scott, Frank Finlay, Angela Pleasence, and Edward Woodward. DVD. Entertainment Partners, Ltd., 1984.

A Christmas Carol. Dir. Edwin L. Marin. Perfs. Reginald Owen, Gene Lockhart, Kathleen Lockhart, and Leo G. Carroll. Warner Home Video, 1938.

A Christmas Carol. Dir. Robert Zemeckis. Perfs. Jim Carrey, Gary Oldman, Colin Firth, Bob Hoskins, and Robin Penn Wright. ImageMovers, 2009.

Anthony, Breznican. "3-D 'Christmas Carol' fits Dickens' Vision." *USA Today* n.d.: Academic Search Complete. EBSCO. Web. 9 Nov. 2009.

Bertman, Stephen. "Dante's Role in the Genesis of Dickens' *A Christmas Carol*." *Dickens Quarterly* 24.3 (2007): 167-175. Academic Search Complete. EBSCO. Web. 5 Oct. 2009.

Comte-Sponville, André. *A Small Treatise on the Great Virtues: The Uses of Philosophy in Everyday Life.* Trans. Catherine Temerson. New York: Metropolitan Books/Henry Holt and Company, 2001.

Dickens, Charles. *A Christmas Carol and Other Holiday Tales.* Ann Arbor: Borders Classics, 2006.

Eirik, Sten. "Humbug: Apperceptions of a Controller." *Individual Psychology: The Journal of Adlerian Theory, Research & Practice* 53.1 (1997): 81-88. Academic Search Complete. EBSCO. Web. 18 Jan. 2010.

Epstein, Norrie. "A Christmas Carol." *The Friendly Dickens: Being a Good-Natured Guide to the Art and Adventures of the Man Who Invented Scrooge.* New York: Viking Penguin, 1998. 174-192.

Henson, Brian, dir. *The Muppet Christmas Carol*. Audio commentary. DVD. Jim Henson Productions, 1993.

Kleinberg, Aviad. *7 Deadly Sins: A Very Partial List*. Trans. Susan Emanuel. Cambridge: The Belknap Press of Harvard University Press, 2008.

Mickey's Christmas Carol. Dir. Burny Mattinson. Perfs. Alan Young, Wayne Allwine, Hal Smith, and Clarence Nash. Walt Disney Productions, 1983.

The Muppet Christmas Carol. Dir. Brian Henson. Perfs. Michael Caine, Frank Oz, Dave Gomez. DVD. Jim Henson Productions, 1993.

Newey, Vincent. "A Christmas Carol: Snatched?" *The Scriptures of Charles Dickens: Novels of Ideology, Novels of the Self*. Burlington: Ashgate, 2004. 17-55.

Plato. "Apology." *The Last Days of Socrates*. Trans. Hugh Tredennick and Harold Tarrant. London: Penguin Books, 2003.

Scrooge. Dir. Ronald Neame. Perfs. Albert Finney, Edith Evans, Kenneth More, and Alec Guiness. DVD. Waterbury Films, 1970.

Beauty Witness

Jobie Watson
Howard County Community College

> *Editors' Note:* The great snowstorm of 2010 dropped over two feet of snow in the Baltimore area in February 2010.

I am sole witness to a million little pieces of beauty every day: sunrise and sunset, blooming flowers and falling leaves, the sound of rain and the song of birds. It's amazing, but I don't think I notice them. Worse yet, in my ineptitude at witnessing beauty with my eyes or ears, I miss the opportunity to participate in it. Do I compromise the beauty in each of these little moments because I fail to experience it as anything other than annoyance or pain? Shouldn't I look at each as a graceful or stunning moment?

I'm not a fan of winter and didn't particularly appreciate SnowKahuna[1] this year. A few days after the big snowfall, I was at work when I heard familiar coo-hooing. When I looked out the workplace window and saw nothing, I thought of home in Alabama where my mother has a bird clock that chimes twelve different birdsongs. I'm sure that in some universe it's beautiful, though when at home I'm tempted to pop the batteries out of that clock. At seven o'clock there is a mourning dove. I know mourning doves are out there; I can hear them. I'm wishing, like at home, I had a BB gun and a clear shot; but the windows are sealed and I don't have

Jobie Watson just graduated from Howard County Community College as a philosophy major. She has a previous degree in Performance from the University of Southern Mississippi. She is making plans to study in a doctoral program. In the meantime, she writes and occasionally directs local theatre productions.

a BB gun. The coo-hooing continues. Later, I walk by the window again and there the two doves sit on a reservoir tank cuddling and preening each other. In my head I throw open the forever-sealed window yelling, "Take it somewhere else or shut it, will ya!"

I should be horrified at my reaction to the beauty I just witnessed. Why can't I appreciate it as a grace-filled announcement? After all, the birds are sensing spring and singing its praises. Spring is my element, spring makes me happy. What isn't praiseworthy about spring? I should be humbled by the invitation to participate as their chosen audience member, their sole eyewitness; but I don't want to hear them. Even as much as I hate winter and long for spring, I would prefer they kept their heartfelt song to themselves. I can experience spring without their welcome-spring-sappy-song. When spring arrives, I can see its sunrise, pick its flowers, and touch my feet to its cool grass. I don't need to get my heart involved to appreciate beauty.

Helen Keller would disagree with me. She said, "The most beautiful things in the world cannot be seen or even touched but must be felt with the heart."

She is a remarkable witness for beauty. I, on the other hand, am a miserable beauty student. As I see it through my own eyes and with my own heart, beauty is often superimposed onto the retina of my heart as irritation or pain.

My violent inclination toward the mourning doves makes me a little ashamed. I know better because I had a chance to learn about being a beauty witness on a very long walk.

Several years ago, I walked across Spain on a pilgrim trail called the Camino de Santiago.

This trail was no respecter of persons. I watched sixty-year-old men and women pass me on the trail and walk kilometers farther than me on a daily basis. I watched as the Camino all but had a professional soccer player crawling on his knees at the end of each day's walk. Me? I was somewhere in between walking and crawling. I can tell you about the pain, the stress and the exhaustion of the trip, because I was there, an eyewitness to it every day.

I may have known I was in good shape before I left for Spain, but I didn't witness that fact on the Camino. Within three days of a five-week journey, an old ankle injury returned with sometimes immobilizing pain; it also caused tendonitis to flare up in my knee. On top of that, it rained the first few days of the trip, constant and heavy. It was cold. In the third week, on Easter in Burgos, it snowed. I won't tell you again what my least favorite season is, but

I will confess that I was unable to foster a good attitude. Even worse, I wasn't able to appreciate the beauty of a moment I will never experience again: snow in Burgos on Easter.

One of the men that I met was from Norway. A family man, he was at least ten years older than me with a steady job. He had two walking poles and he hiked much faster than I could ever dream of moving. The second time I saw him was on a muddy hill outside of Puente la Reina; he walked so fast, he passed me it was as if I was sliding backwards—which, coincidently, I was—covered with red mud.

While I struggled, he embraced; as I limped, he flew. He told me that he did the trail every couple of years. Every time he returned home after walking it, he couldn't watch TV or read the papers, because he couldn't stand the noise. He was a remarkable witness for the escape that the trail offered. His experience of the trail was so deep that he took it back home with him.

I couldn't see anything beyond cold and pain. There was nothing that I wanted to take back with me, nothing like spring's first flower that I wanted to press and preserve.

Does that make the trail painful? Do I trade solace for irritation at less-than-ideal temperatures? And the beauty, where was it when I was there?

When I returned from Spain, one thing I could say about the trip was that it was stressful. Part of that may be because the focus of my mind was always walk, eat, sleep, walk, eat, sleep. I couldn't always walk without pain. When I was hungry, it was often during siesta. I made it a habit of not looking at the sheets I slept in, though the smell was often there to greet me. I brought that stress back with me, which manifested itself in nightmares for over a year. However, there was one blessing that came from the curse of that focus. Since I was a witness to such long days of pain, I also returned with a steady, slow pace, full of a peaceful sense of what I can do and what I can't do. And though I rarely spent time focused in awe and wonder, I can recall brief moments of beauty.

However, I'm afraid that I missed most of it. I looked toward the end of each day for rest and hopefully a clean smelling bed but I rarely looked to the horizon. There were sunsets every day, but until the last week of the five-week trip, I never took the time to see. There were vineyards blooming on hillsides and horses tethered in fields of rolling fog, which I noticed only out of the corner of my eye. I know beauty was there and I know I missed it.

That seems to be a travesty that I practice over and over. I practice embracing the irritation, grasping for the negative instead of welcoming the beautiful. I overload myself with a burden of pain rather than the search for beauty.

What do I have to gain from embracing the negative instead of basking in the beautiful?

If beauty is in the eye of the beholder, as an eyewitness to it I am rather inept, even dumb. It's sad but true: I don't deserve the invitation by a couple of doves to hear their song in praise of spring.

A quote from a famous entertainer comes to mind. And though I probably misrepresent the intention of her quote, I can't help but think that it must apply. Whether my eye is already blackened from my lack of looking or whether instead I deserve it to be blackened, I can't say. This rather beautiful pig seems to have one up on me. I'm sure, if she could, Miss Piggy would say: "Beauty is in the eye of the beholder and it may be necessary from time to time to give a stupid or misinformed beholder a black eye."

Instead of seeking the wisdom of a pig, though, maybe it's time I tried seeing. I could go back to Spain and re-walk those many kilometers between Pamplona and Santiago de Compostela, but yesterday is too late to change. Today is something I have right now. Today it's not too late to squint into the sunshine and smile or press my cheek against a kitten enjoying the comforting smell only sun-warmed kittens have. And then there's tomorrow. It will be a day of a million descriptions, any of which can be beautiful, if I decide to be their sole beauty witness.

Shattered: Collapse of the Twin Towers

Tom Pisciotta
Chesapeake College

I had recently broken up with my college sweetheart in Florida, thrown what possessions I could fit into my Honda and headed to Mom's house on the Eastern shore to get my life back together. My good friend Ben W. got word that I was home and called me up a day later.

"Hey man, how would you like to go to New York to visit my brothers with me? I'd love the company." For the first time in years I feel like I am getting back to my roots. Ben and Dan and Rob always promoted personal expression and I knew a trip with them was just what my soul needed after the wringing out I had had with the breakup. I filled up a large camping backpack with socks, underwear, clothes of all sorts and tied as many buckets as I could onto the pack's straps. If there are two things about me you need to know, one is: I don't travel light; the other is: I drum on plastic buckets everywhere I go.

We formulate a plan that calls for me to meet Ben on the road, leave my car and go with him in his car to my uncle's house in Hoboken. We arrive in fading twilight to the sounds of cicadas and crickets filling the night air with their insect music. From there we hustle to the PATH train. Too late it occurs to me that I am way overpacked. My bag is nearly as big as I am! I feel like one of those

Thomas Pisciotta currently resides on Maryland's Eastern Shore. Under the stage name Tommy Buckets he travels the world bringing his bucket beats and fun-loving attitude with him everywhere he goes. Since his experience in the World Trade Center on 9/11 he has been inspired to study and practice medicine, first as an electroneurodiagnostic technologist, and most recently as a student in Chesapeake College's Radiologic Technologist program. He continues to share his passion for the drums and life in general and enjoys teaching, learning and sharing with everyone he encounters.

World War paratroopers, waddling along with all sorts of gear hanging off the backpack straps. We hop the PATH train into NYC and rumble under the Hudson, arriving in the North Tower's massive underbelly. There we find an elaborate complex of subway junctions punctuated with an underground mall. We arrive late on the night Sept 5th. And most of the shops are closed. I had been hoping to go to the roof and get an eyeful of the New York skyline, and to bust out on the buckets and busk a bit. I love the rich acoustics of buckets in the subway. Fortunately, the buckets have to wait. There is hardly a soul in the subway and we are in a hurry to meet our collected crew. Ben turns to me and in a hushed voice says,

"This is the building the terrorists bombed in '93."

There was much talk of such things at the W. household growing up. Ben's dad was the head of the CIA, responsible for the daily briefing to the president.

We stand in silent awe a moment. I can't imagine what it must have been like for the people standing here when the blast went off. It seems distant now, eight years later. We proceed to our train and head uptown for a few drinks. At first I'm a little down, but the joyous atmosphere of our party rubs off on me. We laugh and joke into the small hours. Dan mentions he has a video camera and we start making plans to make a video we refer to as *Bucketman.* In the video, Bucketman, played by me, does percussion in the subway and the WASP, played by Ben, steals his tips at every turn, forcing Bucketman to confront him and do battle. I put forth the idea of doing the final confrontation at the World Trade Center, and the boys are into it.

Our time passes quickly in the bustling city. There is so much to do and so many friends to see, not to mention performing and filming in between functions. The night of the tenth looms up to cast a shadow on our production. We're sleeping at Ben's brother Dan's place in Brooklyn. I am hoping we can squeeze in the planned shoot at the World Trade Center, but Ben's girlfriend is flying into Reagan National at 6:00 pm the next day, September 11th, and that's all he can focus on.

Ben's brother Dan comes in to say goodnight. Ben outlines the itinerary for the next day. "The plan is to get up early, go to the North Tower accompanied by our videographer Dan, where we will film a final scene of project *Bucketman.* In the scene, Tom's playing buckets in the subway and I put a bucket over his head and steal his tips. Then it's on to the PATH train, back to the car in Newark, and on to Reagan National airport to pick up my girlfriend Sharon."

"What about the rooftop?" I ask. I have always wanted to go to the roof of the WTC and see the New York skyline.

"We'll have to see. I just don't think we'll have time tomorrow," he says.

With that we hit the sheets. We get up bright and early and pack up. Dan loads up his cameras and we all schlep our bags down to the Brooklyn terminal. The three of us stop in for breakfast and coffee at a little diner. Just as we're walking down into the metro Dan's cell rings. He talks to the caller for a minute. Then he addresses us: "Lucky thing I've got all my camera gear with me. That was a modeling agency uptown. They're offering me some photography work. Sorry guys, I gotta take these gigs when I can, so 'Bucket Man' will have to wait." Like many New Yorkers, Dan freelances to supplement his income. I'm disappointed but try not to show it. Just then we hear a train pulling in.

We run down the escalator and slip through the train doors just before they close. We find our seats and in a few moments of the train's gentle rocking I'm nodding in and out, trying to stay awake. An attractive girl with a big portfolio takes the seat next to me. We engage in a conversation about her art, but she is reluctant to open the portfolio. She studies my gargantuan bag, which is hogging up the bulk of two seats, and inquires about the buckets tied to the pack. I begin to tell her about "Bucket Man." She seems less than impressed.

"Come on, Tom. This is our stop!" Ben interrupts, and I'm thankful to disengage from the conversation.

We exit the train and the first thing I notice is how empty the stop is. I was expecting a bustling epicenter of commuters and commerce, raring for a little bucket busking. As far as I could see the only people were maybe two or three other people from our train, and in a moment we are alone. It also seems darker than usual, as though they don't have all the lights on. Ben ushers me upstairs to the PATH train terminal, where the same scene of silent solitude awaits. To add to our confusion there is "Police Line Do Not Cross" tape blocking the turnstiles for the train. We look to one another and begin scanning the area to ask someone what the holdup is about. Finally a Port Authority guard appears near the ticket window and we approach him.

"What are you guys doing? This area is supposed to be cleared!" he yells out, waving us toward the escalator. This makes my ears perk up, and my mind kicks into "journalist mode." I start firing questions at him—"What happened? Did the PATH train derail? Anybody hurt? How long—"

"Evacuate the building now!" comes his curt response, and by his tone we can tell he's not fooling around. We proceed to the escalator. It's not moving, and there are two very heavyset women with a kid in a stroller blocking the bottom.

"My goodness, how do they expect us to get up all them steps this stroller and this child? It's crazy!" the mother says to her companion.

"Need a hand?" I ask. The mother studies me and my bag of buckets for a moment, her eyebrow raised, head cocked slightly to the side as though I had just told her the lead-in to an unhumorous joke.

"No thank you, we're fine," she says. After a considerable delay the mother takes the child out of the stroller and her companion drags it, bumping and jostling slowly and precariously, up the steps, pausing every few feet to catch her breath. Ben and I wait patiently at the bottom so as not to add to their irritation.

Once they get close to the top Ben and I start up the escalator. I'm out of breath when we reach the corridor that leads out of the North Tower. The two ladies are nowhere to be seen. As my eyes adjust to the daylight ahead of me, it becomes apparent that things are very out of the ordinary. The first thing I notice is the huge cylinder standing on end in between us and the South Tower. It's about the size of a cement truck. A ribbon of bright yellow "Police Line Do Not Cross" tape cordons off a square around it. I don't realize until much later that I am looking at the turbine from one of the planes. Behind the cylinder I see people pressed up against the windows of the South Tower, pointing up toward the top of the North Tower. As we come to the mouth of the corridor, our field of vision widens, and we see the plaza is littered with blackened, twisted debris. It's hard to tell what I'm looking at, but I recognize the legs of a desk and what looks like the remains of a suit jacket among the rubble. Our forward progress is halted as a team of firemen loaded down with gear rushes past us and disappears into a stairway in the corridor. The last man in locks eyes with me for a split second and there's sweat running down his cheek. His jaw is set, a look of resignation on his face. Then they're gone into the bowels of the immense building. I turn back toward the light and step out of the corridor, my neck craning back to follow the graceful lines of the South Tower up, up, up, until they are enveloped by black rolling smoke, orange tongues of fire licking at the edge. There are white papers floating lazily every which way, like some sort of ghastly ticker-tape parade. My heart races, my face burning with the rush of adrenaline and I realize not only is the South Tower on fire, but above us the North Tower is billowing smoke as well.

A terrifying smack on the pavement draws my attention to the left. Something has plummeted to earth on the other side of the fire truck parked maybe fifty feet away, narrowly missing several paramedics and firemen who are unloading.

I hear their anguished cries, "Damn! Move! Move!"

My brain is reeling. I can't fathom what is happening. The only lucid thought I have is, "Did we just walk out onto a movie set?"

Ben claps a hand on my shoulder. "The terrorists! They've come back to New York!"

We are smack in the middle of the south side of the North Tower. I realize we are going to have to run the gauntlet of falling debris. We look to the right and it's an impossibly long way to go. To the left toward the vehicles and the open space of the plaza seems like the right choice. Ben is already headed that way. I keep my eyes on him and follow his lead, trying to dodge the rubble, puddles, and obstacles as we move past them. Though we're rounding the southeast corner of the North Tower in a moment, it feels like we're moving in slow motion. It is like in a nightmare where you can't move quickly enough and you awaken with your legs tangled in the sheets. I keep hoping I'll wake up but the nagging weight of my bag, the noise and calamity is all too real. We emerge from the confining space between the two buildings, into the plaza. There are people ahead of us. There is an immense sculpture off to our right. Finally we reach the first real street. There are no cars on the road and almost no cars parked within sight. Sirens scream as ambulances and fire trucks push through the crowded streets toward us. There's a cop on the corner across from us directing the flow of human traffic.

"Uptown, uptown! Everyone go uptown. Away from the towers!" A line of onlookers behind him stare, transfixed and deaf to his commands.

A figure breaks from the crowd toward the plaza. The officer whirls around and grabs the man by the collar. I'm close enough to reach out and touch them.

"You can't go down there!"

"But I'm a—" The man stops mid-sentence, his eyes wide, mouth agape. Gasps and screams erupt from the crowd.

The cop points up over my shoulder toward the towers.

"Ruuunnn!" he commands.

The sea of people whirl on their heels and erupt uptown. I look back over my shoulder, following the line of the officer's arm. The top quarter of the South Tower is tearing from its foundation and is canted toward us. The crowd in front of me surges forward like runners in a marathon at the starting gate. The rumble behind us is deafening. Ben is in front of me and the distance between us grows as he zigzags though the crowd. Fortunately he's got his gym bag above his head to fit through the crowd. As hard as I'm pushing, the corners of my bag are holding me, caught between the people to my right and left. My only thought is to drop the pack and win the race for survival. I tear at the straps and manage to release a few of the buckets, but the main straps, having been knotted together, then pulled taut by my exertions, are impossible. In fact the crowd is practically pulling me along, and I have no control over the path I take. For a moment I'm running with one foot up on the sidewalk, one foot in the street, and have to dodge a few light poles and a trash can. The can is quivering, literally shaking with the force of the floors of the South Tower falling to the ground. The sound is palpable now, its intensity pulsing, undulating as each story implodes onto the one below it, faster and faster into a nerve-shattering roar. An older lady stumbles and goes down ahead of me to the right. I ready myself to pull her up as I'm dragged past, but the people in her immediate vicinity pull her back onto her feet.

I'm the better part of the way down the first block when I dare to look back. What I see is a tidal wave, a fluid volcanic flow of debris shooting down the street right for us! It has engulfed the plaza and is cascading past the North Tower. The crowd behind us is thin, and a few people back at the bottom of the block on the other side of the street jump into doorways to escape being swallowed up. The stuff is practically boiling down the street. My only thought is, *run faster!*

I struggle to spot Ben. I think I spot his bag at the top of the block but I'm not sure.

A geyser of grey gas comes shooting out of the sewer in front of me. With the crowd thick around me I'm forced to go through it. I take a deep breath, hoping it's not poisonous or caustic, and plunge through its periphery. I come out the other side intact. I'm not sure if the people behind are pushing on me, if fear is propelling me, but I could practically feel the stuff shoving me from behind like a strong wind. I'm running faster than I've ever run in my life! Barreling into the intersection, I'm scanning the area where I last saw Ben. I'm about to break down, feeling that if I lose him it's all over for me. I'm scanning the path he would have taken up Broadway, but I see no gym bag. A few people are cutting left to get onto the side street. The dust is upon us now, washing everything out in a thick grey blanket. In a moment I won't be able to see my own shoes. I look to the north corner and there's someone scanning the crowd as it rushes by. He meets my gaze and thank god, there's Ben, waiting for me.

"This way!" he commands. The dust comes swirling into the intersection on Broadway. Ben turns the corner and we cut west on the side street, which is less crowded. My legs are burning and my heart's hammering in my chest. By the time we get to the next corner we're sort of jogging. I'm on the verge of collapse.

"Hold up, hold up, I gotta slow down." I'm panting. We walk for a moment. The enveloping dust is still creeping along behind us, but with the wind pulling it to the east it is thinning out. I elbow my cumbersome bag. "I gotta learn to travel a little lighter! Dig into the side pockets here for a bottle of water."

We pass it back and forth. Ben takes out his cell phone. "I'm going to call my parents and let them know we're alive." He presses the phone to his ear.

There's a payphone up ahead of us with a line of people waiting to use it, but the line's moving fast. I start groping in my pockets for change. Two people emerge out of the dust behind us and come into view. The woman catches my eye first. She's a very attractive lady, dirty blonde in a business suit skirt and form-fitting jacket. She's not very dusty. What catches my eye are her legs. She's got at least one long gash across her leg which is going to need some serious stitches, with blood pouring down from it and a few smaller wounds.

"Lady, you better sit down," I say, gesturing to her leg. She's been stressed past the point of dissociation and shows no sign of stopping. Some other people notice her. An authoritative bespectacled gentleman steps forward and takes charge.

"We need something clean to press on that wound!" He says to the crowd and a packet of tissues is produced. "There's a hospital up the street," the gentleman says to her. She seems to be just now taking notice of her wounds.

"But I have to get home ... they'll be so worried," she says, and the rest is lost as he takes her in the direction of the hospital.

Ben's getting no service on the cell phone. Another man who has come through the thick of the dust has caught up. He looks like he's been rolled in flour. His shoes, pants, jacket, briefcase, face, and hair are grey-white. His glasses are so dusty I can't see his eyes and he practically runs into us. Having grown up wearing bifocals, I instinctively go to help him.

"How can you see out of those? Here, wipe them on my shirt," I say. He exposes his slightly less dismal undershirt, wipes them, then I take them. His eyes are red and bleary. I put a few drops of water on my shirt to clean the glasses more thoroughly. He studies the bottle ravenously. "Here." I hand it to him, feeling rude to not offer.

He tips his head back and pours the water into his eyes to wash out the grit, then swishes a bit in his mouth. "Thanks. I'm Jim. Jim McMahon."

He sticks his hand out and we shake. "I'm Tom. Tommy Buckets. Nice to meet you," I say. I edge back over to the line for the phone so I don't lose my spot.

"Well, thanks and good luck," says Jim, nodding to the phone, and he continues uptown.

In a moment it's my turn at the phone. I slap the change into the slot, put the receiver to my ear, and there are already people on the phone. A lot of people all talking at once, saying "Hello, hello, Suzan? *Holá, e Pablo estas?* Who is this? Hello, hello?" The lines must be crossed, the system is down. I push the change return and try to get my finger into the slot, but the door is already blocked by all the change that people have left behind. Bewildered, I hand the phone to the guy behind me as Ben approaches.

"I couldn't get through. No service," Ben says, holding up his phone.

"Me neither—we're cut off. We gotta make it up to Union Square. My cousin's in the dorm up there and we've got other friends there as well," I remind Ben. He nods. Up ahead near a big construction trash bin some people are gathered around a radio. Its loud blaring becomes audible. "... Reports are pouring in from all over but information is spotty right now, but it seems that at least one aircraft has struck the World Trade Center. The Pentagon has also been struck by an aircraft which is believed to have been a commuter jet ..."

Ben is wide-eyed, the color draining from his face. "My dad is at a meeting at the Pentagon," he says to me.

The whispering scream of an aircraft engine perforates the air.

"Here comes another one!" Somebody yells. People run for cover. Ben and

I crouch beside the bin. My mind reels with what I just heard. I crane my neck skyward and see a blue streak overhead.

"F-18 Eagle. It's one of ours!" One of the construction guys yells. I breathe a sigh of relief.

A guy in a suit comes out of a building and yells out in the direction of the payphone: "If you're trying to use the phone we have an open line in here. You're welcome to come in and use it."

Ben and I look to the man, then to each other, and we're on our way. Ben goes up the stairs into the building first. The security guy lets Ben past, but jumps up when he sees me.

"Stop right there!"

"Sorry. I'm with him," I say, gesturing to Ben. "The man outside said we could use the phone."

"Oh, I just seen you tearing in here with that big bag … You look a little… I'm just not taking any chances." He pats his sidearm and resumes his perch on a stool.

Ben is seated at a workbench with a row of phones. There are several benches with more phones. There are massive computer banks, wires snaking into tight bundles and crisscrossing the room.

I pick up a phone and there's the old familiar dial tone. I punch in the number and the phone lady responds. "All circuits are busy … Please try your call again later."

I get the same answer on my second try. Third try and the phone is ringing! My exhilaration is quickly dashed when I get the machine. "Figures, World War Three and my folks don't answer," I snicker to myself. I leave a rambling message, something to the effect of, "Hey Ma, Ben and I are fine. If you could call his parents and see how they are and tell them everybody's all right, that'd be great. We're going to keep moving uptown to Union Square since the fires are spreading and all the fire trucks and all the stuff is wrecked. I'll call you when I can. Love ya. I hope you're ok."

We come out of the building and everyone's looking downtown. My heart sinks as I realize there is nothing visible left of the South Tower.

"Look, there goes another one," someone says. I strain my eyes and see a tiny form plummet from a window high on the North Tower. A lady with a stylish brimmed hat turns her head and crosses herself. A man with a video camera tracks the figure from the building to the ground. I can't believe what I'm seeing. A moment later the same voice calls out, "There go two at a time. They look like they're holding hands." The lady beside me is wringing her hands, tears coming down.

"Oh my God! Oh my God. What have they done?"

Another man approaches the cameraman, who is eating up the horrific scene unfolding in front of us with his lens. I figure he's going to say something about human decency, but instead he says, "I work for NBC. I need that camera. How much do you want for it?"

The cameraman unflinchingly films the horror unfolding, "Nah, man, I got footage, I got lots of good footage on this tape," he says.

"Eight thousand, how's eight thousand sound? Company check." The agency man produces his checkbook and is waving it in the man's face.

"I was thinking more like…"

The man whispers in the agent's ear, and he begins scribbling on the checkbook. I feel like I'm going to barf and have to resist the urge to scream at the two men. We meander back toward the radio. We pause to listen to the journalists struggling to describe the events that are unfolding live before us. I see the agent with the camera way down the block running toward the beacon of smoke, dust and ash. Then the North Tower lets loose a rumbling bellow and begins to unravel, crashing down with a thunderous rumble and an eruption of dust and ash. The last thing I see is the shattered fingers of the bright metal façade jutting up from the imploded bottom floors. Then the surge of dust blocks everything out again.

The woman in the hat is sobbing into her hands. A wave of woeful gasps, screams, and shrieks surround me. Instinctively we resume our trek uptown. We come to a beautiful brick building which looks like a school of some sort. There are the first trees I'm aware of seeing. They seem particularly beautiful today. The people in the brick building have flung open their doors. They have tables out by the street with rows of cups of water. They are bandaging limbs, rinsing eyes, giving aid to those seeking refuge from the tempest of destruction that has enveloped the southern flank of Manhattan. All the way up the street the scene repeats itself. New Yorkers have thrown aside their better-safe-than-sorry, street-savvy attitude toward humanity and are opening their doors and offering aid to people they've never met before.

We pause for water at the booth. Ben asks where the hospital is.

"What are you doing? You hurt?" I ask him.

"No but I'm O negative, the universal donor for transfusions. I'm going to give blood. I know they're going to need it."

"Something else we might need is money. I'd like to get some out of the machine if we see one," I add.

A few blocks further up we find a bank machine with a line maybe twelve deep to make withdrawals. The guy three people in front of us is a dignified Middle Eastern man with a turban and beard. His turban, coupled with his height, makes him stand out. We are joined by two thick-necked, red-faced guys with city accents.

"You know who it is, it's the f—king Arabs who did this. They're gonna pay! Man they're gonna pay!" the one guy says to the other. The other guy is not so loud, but he's helping to work the loud guy up to a boil. We're trying to ignore them, as is the fellow in the turban who glances back nervously when they're particularly loud or vulgar. They find an audience in a third man who comes up and affirms their boisterous claims. Then, like the leader of a wolf pack, the loud guy surges up, snapping at the man with the turban: "You happy now, Muhammed? Eh Ack-med! You happy with what you did?" The man is pushing up on Ben and me, yelling and gesticulating in the direction of the cloud of smoke. No one is offering resistance. The rest of the line turns their heads in indifference. I look to Ben and he springs into action.

"Look at this guy! Does he look like a threat to you? Does he look like the guy who did this?"

You can see the loud guy reeling a bit, trying to come up with what he's going to say, so I jump in, too, to cut him off and help drown him out.

"You think this guy would stick around if he had something to do with this? This guy's a New Yorker, same as the rest of us! And he's scared, same as the rest of us. Now could we just have some peace while we're waiting for the machine?"

Enough of the crowd nods their approval for the guy to back down, but he's still audible behind us. After a few more tense minutes the guy with the turban is on his way, as are Ben and I. We stop by a pizzeria and order a slice. Everything inside is so ordinary looking that I feel like I've come out of the nightmare.

"How's it going?" I ask the guy behind the counter.

He stares at me incredulously for a moment.

"Terrible, absolutely terrible. My brother's missing, along with most of his ladder company. I'm trying to think of what I'm going to say to his wife and kid. Everything is in the toilet, and I'm stuck here at work 'cause nobody else will come in so I can get outta here. Sorry, I don't mean to snap, but ..."

He turns back to the oven with the slices and I feel like it would have been less obtrusive to kick myself in the head before putting my foot in my mouth. I sit down with Ben in silence, picking at the knots in my bag's ties, working them loose. I close my eyes and see that firefighter's face again, eyes fixed with the look of stolid determination, the sweat coming down. Could he have known, as he looked up at the fuming hulk of the Twin Towers, if today would be his last day? Did he think of his family, his wife, daughter, brother or sister as he started up? The corners of my eyes fill up and I try to think of something, anything else. Our pizza comes up but my appetite is lost. We nibble a bit, then chuck the remnants and head up to our friends' apartment. The entrance door is open, as is their apartment door. I am grateful to get my pack off and stow it. We tune into the news, which is on every channel. Ben breathes a sigh of relief when his dad is mentioned on TV.

"My dad is on in ten minutes to give a press conference, so it looks like he's OK."

This brings a much-needed breath of levity into the atmosphere. Family members are being located and the pieces begin coming back together, although for more than a few there are gaping holes where people are missing. After the conference, I walk Ben to the hospital. I'm prepared to give blood as well but the line is around the block. Ben announces his blood type to someone at the triage center and he is immediately rushed to the front of the line.

"I'll see you back at the place!" he yells over his shoulder, and he's off.

I mull about near the hospital until I locate my cousin's dorm. He's surprisingly easy to get a hold of on the phone at the security desk. We go up to the roof to get a look around. Battered vehicles are being towed uptown, shedding a wake of dust behind them. Newly arrived, polished fire trucks and ambulances stream downtown in their stead. Another plume of dust rises as a smaller building adjoining the Trade Center gives way and collapses. I'm exhausted, and pretty soon I hunker down in the dorm as the news coverage drones on. A bottle is produced and passed around and the conversation turns to what the future will bring. War is the key word. We offer a prayer for those who died and a prayer that war will not be the outcome. Later that night, as a retaliatory cruise missile strike is reported, we realize our sophomoric stance. The knee jerk reaction of fear and anger overwhelms the urge to understand how or why such a thing might happen. For the people that saw the face of carnage close up, whether it's a cruise missile or a Boeing 676, I can only hope they would never will such an episode on other people.

So that about wraps it up. I feel like I should wax philosophical but I can't seem to. Here's where I was going.

It's our shame that our first instinct to follow our pain with the pain of others. Hate is a boiling infection that consumes one's identity and spreads through contact. Cool it.

Open Submissions

Middle-Text: Orality and Literacy in *Middlesex*

Melissa Pankake
Ursinus College

After the familiar invocation to the Muse, the beginning of Homer's *Odyssey* contains a particular line that has often given translators trouble: τῶν ἁμόθεν γε, θεά, θύγατερ Διός, εἰπὲ καὶ ἡμῖν (I.10): literally, "Of these things, goddess, daughter of Zeus, tell us too." The line implies that others have already heard "these things" many times, and that "we," readers from ancient Greece to the present-day U.S.A., are at the end—or the middle, or anywhere but the beginning—of a grand, unfathomable tradition. But the modern reader may not feel the full scope of this statement. An ideology of textuality now dominates, leading us to make certain assumptions about an oral epic that we see in written form. For example, we assume a single author (Homer, who is probably a mythic retrojection, with an allegorical name that means "singer"), a single date and location of composition (in fact the very language of epic, Attic Greek, is a hybrid dialect, not spoken in any region of Greece but intelligible in every region), and unity of the final product (Homer's epics are littered with spurious lines that one singer may have added while another omitted). We wish to believe that the text is fixed and solid and free of ambiguity. However, works rooted in the oral tradition cannot be represented accurately when we are operating under an ideol-

Melissa Pankake is completing her undergraduate career at Ursinus College, studying English and Classics. She hopes to pursue a Masters of Arts degree in Medieval English Literature and continue her work on concepts of authorship and the oral tradition.

ogy of textuality. Oral tradition morphs, changes, and fluctuates; it is allowed to change its mind, remake itself, and embrace its own ambiguous nature. It is constantly updating according to its context. Clearly, Jeffrey Eugenides's novel *Middlesex* does not function as an oral song. It is a printed text with a definite author and fixed date of composition. However, *Middlesex* is also a hybrid novel, existing in the form of a printed text but drawing on the oral tradition. The narrator Cal, himself a hybrid, presents his story in text but also longs for the more active communicative style of oral tradition. Finally, *Middlesex* rejects an essentialist concept of gender as connected to biological sex (which is aligned with an ideology of the authority of text and reliance upon the printed word) in favor of a fluid, changeable, hybridized and hybrid-embracing concept of gender as performance (aligned with the more fluid ideology of oral tradition).

In *Middlesex*, Eugenides hybridizes written text and oral performance. The hybridization begins in the second sentence: "specialized readers may have come across me in Dr. Peter Luce's study" (3). Cal demonstrates awareness of his audience's eclectic, heterogeneous nature, while simultaneously acknowledging that he, the narrator, has been and is now located upon a printed page; the narrator is textualized, but it is almost as if he is speaking to his audience from the printed page. Cal also adopts a highly narrative style, switching his tense from past to present in moments of suspense or important action (11, 15, 32, 53-55, 210), as often occurs in epic narrative literature. He attempts to make his story vivid and visual, directing the reader to "look" (63) rather than simply relying on his words. Throughout the novel, the author actively tries to create an impression of the narrator as a storyteller. As Cal resumes his narrative in the beginning of the second chapter, he states. "I have to pick up where explosions interrupted me yesterday" (42), creating the illusion that his narration is unedited stream-of-consciousness and that each chapter represents a day-long session of storytelling.

The specific variety of oral literature that *Middlesex* invokes is the epic. It opens with the unmistakable invocation to the Muse: "Sing now, O Muse, of the recessive mutation on my fifth chromosome!" (4). We might gloss over this invocation—sweeping it up along with the *in medias res* introduction, the narrative-consuming flashbacks and disregard for linear temporality, the lengthy digressions, and the proleptic bits—and assume that it is only there to elicit a chuckle from the reader. According to Bahktin, the noticeable adoption of another's discourse and its interpellation into "common" discourse has a necessarily comic effect (679); perhaps that is all Eugenides had in mind. But, of course, Bahktin has also noted that there is no such thing as neutral speech, and that we must seek out context in order to understand fully anything an author writes. Eugenides's choice to invoke the Muse in recognizably Homeric fashion points to the hybrid nature of *Middlesex* as both oral epic and literary novel. Presumably, the particular Muse that Eugenides seeks to invoke is the same one whom Homer implored: Calliope, the Muse of epic poetry (Smith). While Calliope's realm was typically the oral poem, she is portrayed by later artists carrying a writing tablet; thus, she covers both oral and written literature, and might be perceived as a mediating figure between them. And we cannot miss that "Calliope" is also the name of our narrator and protagonist for the first seventeen years of his life. Calliope, the guardian of the liminal space between oral poem and text, shares her name with the narrator of a story that occupies that space.[1] The narrator is invoking himself. This fascinating maneuver brings home the hybrid concept of authorship in *Middlesex*: the novel is both Muse-inspired (part of a fluid tradition) and authored (a fixed text), for the Muse and the author are one and the same.

In "The Storyteller," Walter Benjamin sums up the disparity between orality and literacy:

> What distinguishes the novel from the story (and from the epic in the narrower sense) is its essential dependence on the book.... What can be handed on orally, the wealth of the epic, is of a different kind from what constitutes the stock in trade of the novel. What differentiates the novel from all other forms of prose literature—the fairy tale, the legend, even the novella—is that it neither comes from oral tradition nor goes into it. This distinguishes it from storytelling in particular. The storyteller takes what he tells from experience—his own or that reported by others. And he in turn makes it the experience of those who are listening to his tale. The novelist has isolated himself. (3)

By equating the "author" with the Muse, *Middlesex* begins to cross the

---

[1] It should be said that Helen, Calliope's middle name, invokes Helen of Troy, a lonely and homeless figure who precariously occupied the space between Troy and Greece, Paris and Menelaus, love and marriage.

boundary between the novel and epic. Although Cal does begin the novel in an isolated position, he soon progresses from the role of distant narrator to that of active participant in his own story: "I can't just sit back and watch from a distance anymore.... Already the world feels heavier, now I'm a part of it" (217). Cal refuses to remain isolated in the position of a novel's narrator; he takes on the role of storyteller. Cal describes the feeling of telling a tale from experience: "I'm talking about bandages and sopped cotton, the smell of mildew in movie theaters, and of all the lousy cats and their stinking litterboxes, of rain on city streets when the dust comes up" (217). Not only does this describe "America" as Cal experiences it, but it is also a metaphor for the "heavier" feeling he described earlier. The smells and sensations are close and crowding; they invoke rooms full of men sweating in the hot Grecian summer, gathered to tell and listen to stories. They describe the very opposite of artistic isolation and of the clean, pure, unambiguous printed word as our lens of textuality would perceive it. As Cal ends the digression and dips back into his story, he concludes: "here we are, at last" (217). For "we," the readers, are now with him and he is with us. He is not our novelist but our storyteller; we are not his readers but his audience, and he feels us gathered around him, listening, as close as the "smell of mildew in movie theaters."

In the handful of moments in the text where Cal directly addresses the reading audience, the oral tradition comes through most powerfully, and most poignantly. Cal laments that "writing is solitary, furtive" (319). Indeed, as our study of oral tradition has shown, writing is a lonely process. The performative aspect is lacking; while texts may retain the shadow of orality, they lose the ability to hold a dialogue with the audience. The readers may feel spoken to by the story, but, in this form, the story can never speak back. Cal, while working through a textual medium, desires the more active, communicative qualities of the oral tradition: "I feel you out there, reader. This is the only kind of intimacy I'm comfortable with. Just the two of us, here in the dark" (319). The storyteller is not the only one who suffers when the medium of storytelling loses its personal human qualities—the audience suffers isolation as well. According to Benjamin, "a man listening to a story is in the company of the storyteller; even a man reading one shares this companionship. The reader of a novel, however, is isolated, more so than any other reader" (10). The ideology of textuality ensures that the reader need never come in contact with the writer, isolating both of them on opposite ends of the communication process.

By invoking the oral tradition, Cal begins to break down the barriers separating reader and writer.

The ideology of textuality fosters a limited view of the uses of language as well. According to Walter Ong, "chirographic cultures regard speech as more specifically informational than do oral cultures, where speech is more performance-oriented, more a way of doing something to someone... the written text appears *prima facie* to be a one-way informational street" (177). Writing is a reduced form of language—with all of the performance elements stripped, only the dry bones of pure information remain.[2] When a culture begins to rely on writing and gets used to this reduced perception of language, a reduced perception of communication results: performance, instead of giving life to the language, becomes an expendable extra element. The ideology is also the source of our modern—for it is quite modern—concept of authorship, which "tends to feel a work as 'closed', set off from other works, a unit in itself. Print culture gave birth to the romantic notions of 'originality' and 'creativity', which set apart an individual work from other works even more" (Ong 133). To our textually centered minds, the author has become a distant, almost mythological figure worthy of reverence: he[3] alone wields the power of creation. Any borrowing from the almighty author is castigated as plagiarism. The role of the audience in the creation of the story, and the story's natural fluctuation in the context of oral tradition, is forgotten. But, as Bahktin reminds us, every word we use is essentially plagiarized from previous language-users. Language is never merely "unitary," reducible to a set of rules and forms that communicate basic information, and is certainly never "neutral": instead, language is a performance, inseparable from its context (674). By borrowing from and invoking other sources and traditions—not only Homer's epics, but also Ovid's *Metamorphoses* and Shakespeare's tragedies—and inviting the reader to participate in the story (as he does most powerfully at the novel's conclusion), Eugenides denies that *Middlesex* or any other novel can ever be "closed."

Another effect of the ideology of textuality is that the written word develops authority, and its power is predictably phallic. For centuries—the pivotal

---

2   Writing can, of course, be beautiful, meaningful, and powerful as well—"reduced" does not necessarily mean "limited." I only mean that, from the perspective of language-as-performance which dominates oral tradition, a written text is the skeleton of a linguistic performance.

3   Indeed, normally a man: see the following paragraph.

centuries during the formation of the western concept of literacy—the ability to write, specifically as it related to chirographic (non-spoken) languages like Latin and ancient Greek, was an exclusively male pursuit (Ong 93; 114). Hélène Cixous connected this to the male-oriented nature of language itself, which "has been governed by the phallus" (881). Even in *Middlesex*, this at first appears to hold true: Lefty is able to read and write in both English and ancient Greek (now exclusively chirographic even to those fluent in modern Greek). Desdemona, on the other hand, is limited to modern Greek and cannot read English, which hinders her ability to understand and be understood in writing without Lefty's help (194). But the male domination over written language does not persist into the next generation: "Though he continued to speak Greek to his parents, Milton never succeeded in writing it, and as he got older he began to forget what even the simplest words meant" (191). Although Lefty has a stronger command of the written word than does Desdemona, the authority of that word turns out to be comparatively empty. Lefty is turned down for a job as a translator—his dominance of the chirographic realm will never make money. Nevertheless, Lefty "spent hours translating Homer and Mimnermos into English. He used beautiful, much too expensive Milanese notebooks and wrote with a fountain pen filled with emerald ink" (131). He continues to treat the writing ritualistically, as though it exercises a special power. When Lefty, deprived of his ability to speak, returns to translations from ancient Greek and to a reliance on writing, there is no power in his utterances. His attempt to comfort Milton with a Greek verse falls on deaf ears (234).

When men discover the emptiness of the written word's phallic authority, the effect is always poignant. Dr. Philobosian is most deluded by the illusory power of the written word. He is convinced that the letter of protection—the very word "protection," which he reads emphatically to himself again and again—would indeed be powerful enough to protect (47; 55). After the soldiers pierce and violate both the document itself and the people it was supposed to defend, the doctor can only think of one explanation: "They couldn't read. They were illiterate!"(61). We do not know whether the soldiers could not read, did not read, or read and ignored. We have only the symbolism of the pierced document, the written "*protection*" powerless to perform the act of protection. The written word, divorced from performance, is dead, deprived of its phallic power.

Although Cixous encouraged her female readers to write because "writing is precisely the very possibility of change" (897), my above statements about the ineffectuality of the written word are not necessarily inconsistent with her theory. For her, feminine writing was very much like the oral tradition: fluid, communicative, visual, gesticulated, and interactive. It, more than male speech and writing, is based on performance. Cixous claims that female speech and writing do not contain "that scission, that division made by the common man between the logic of oral speech and the logic of the text" (881). According to Cixous, the specific "element which never stops resonating, which, once we've been permeated by it, profoundly and imperceptibly touched by it, retains the power of moving us—that element is the song" (881).[4] Feminine writing represents change and empowerment because it has not lost its connection with the oral song and the performative tradition, and because it uses the written word as a communicative tool rather than leaning on it as a crutch.

This is the message in *Middlesex* as well. The printed word is not inherently ineffectual, but divorcing it from performance robs it of power. Through the power of Lefty's (oral) performance of an indignant Frenchman, he obtains the (written) passports that save his and Desdemona's lives (61). Cal also perceives how the written word by itself is insufficient to convey the intricacies of human feeling that might be expressed through performance: "the best proof that the language is patriarchal is that it oversimplifies feeling. I'd like to have at my disposal complicated hybrid emotions ... I've never had the right words to describe my life, and now ... I need them more than ever" (217). Cixous's female writing promises to remarry the written word and the expressive performance, and to restore the empathetic audience-based storytelling of the past; her essay ends with the words "in one another we will never be lacking" (893). Cixous's feminine writing would reconnect the storyteller to the audience, and restore their system of mutual reliance. *Middlesex* is pursuing this dream too.

---

4   From this discussion of Cixous, we might be tempted to draw a parallel between the textual elements of *Middlesex* as "masculine" and the oral tradition elements as "feminine," thus reducing the hybridity of the novel to a restatement of Cal's hybrid gender. But it is too reductive to say that one medium is masculinized while the other is feminized (in fact, oral tradition is a male-dominated realm too, no less so than written tradition). The point is that both media play a role in *Middlesex* and one loses its authority without the other. Tessie's communication with Father Mike, in which she invents a fictitious saintly life for herself while acting very differently, shows that female characters also render the printed word invalid when they divorce it from meaningful corresponding performance—although in Tessie's case, this disconnect was intentional.

The written word, which in the ideology of textuality becomes all-important, is only a signifier. As Ong explained: "Written words are residue. Oral tradition has no such residue or deposit. When an often-told story is not actually being told, all that exists of it is the potential in certain human beings to tell it" (11). Textuality creates a mentality in which words exist even when they are not being pronounced, whereas in reality sounds are over as soon as they are uttered (Ong 91). According to Judith Butler, this is the case with gender as well: it has no life or existence beyond its performance. For this reason, regarding gender as a biologically based certainty (like a text) is an error and a misrepresentation. Gender is more like an oral poem: fluid and changing through time, societies, and even the careers of individual performers. Gender is not "expressive" of sex because it does not exist before it is performed; instead it is created in performance (907-908).

Middlesex substantiates the framework that both gender and the word exist meaningfully only when performed. Every character in *Middlesex* performs, and most are guilty of over-performing, but Cal's performance repertoire is the broadest. Tessie goes "overboard" in making the infant Calliope feminine (224); to an equal extent, Cal later controls his own performance of the male gender (232). With regard to his masculine swagger, Cal comments that "its very falseness made it credible" (449)—gendered acts are fake by definition. The over-the-top performance of one gender or the other creates the illusion of a dichotomous sex-gender system, but the ubiquity of hermpahrodites, metrosexuals (like the purse-swinging Father Mike), and intersexuals in *Middlesex* makes it clear that both gender and, to some extent, biological sex are gradated. The dichotomy, if there is one, is not between male and female, but between a biologically-innate dual sex-gender framework (which corresponds to the Bakhtinian "unitary" concept of language and the fixed ideology of text), and a performance-based sex-gender cline (corresponding to a performance-based concept of language).

The pronouncements that others make about Callie's sexual and gender identity are in written form: Dr. Luce's report and the entry in the Webster's dictionary. Callie rebels against their fixedness. Her—or his—identity cannot be confined to paper; it surpasses the bounds of textuality (and of pronouns). Words are inadequate to define Cal's identity: "I've never had the right words to describe my life, and now ... I need them more than ever" (217). Near the end of the novel, Cal says that "even now, though I live as a man, I remain in essential ways Tessie's daughter" (520). This is not a contradiction—Cal's identity is not fixed and does not have to exist on one side or another of a dichotomy between male and female. Cal freely performs man and daughter; he is the bard, creating his own story in the process of performance. Most importantly, his method of performance is open to change; Cal says that his experiences in Dr. Luce's clinic "pull[ed] her out of line, saying, 'Stay there. Don't move'" (424). This was the root of the trauma: not that Cal's gender identity was threatened with change, but that it was threatened with stability, restriction, and forcible definition on a printed page. Hence the reliance on oral tradition: it is unnatural for Cal to restrict his own gender identity by affixing it to text. He recognizes that text is an unnatural medium for discussing performance-based, fluctuating, constantly changing things like gender and identity: "I, even now, persist in believing that these black marks on white paper bear the greatest significance, that if I keep writing I might be able to catch the rainbow of consciousness in a jar" (297). As soon as Cal has finished trying to write down who he is, he has already changed. Print cannot caput the phenomenon of identity. As a hybrid of oral tradition and text, *Middlesex* is the necessary and inevitable vehicle for portraying the contradiction inherent in restricting unstable gender identity with stable definitions.

The abrupt ending of the novel reveals its hybrid nature. Cal concludes his story "thinking about what was next," thus inviting the reader to consider with him where the story might go from there. In class, we expressed almost universal surprise that the novel ended on such an open note, and left behind so many questions. We wanted to know more about Cal's experiences in college, why he joined the Foreign Service, and how his family and friends reacted to his decision to live as a man. We wanted to know what happened to Julie Kikuchi, and why Cal decided not to try to find the Obscure Object again. And, even though the novel had gone on for over five hundred pages and had spanned a staggering amount of time and space, we wanted to know what came next. If only *Middlesex* really were presented as part of the oral tradition, in which the whims of the audience dictate the length of the story! In societies that still have them, oral stories may be almost infinitely long; if the audience remains attentive, one song may last for months (Lord 16-17). The story is always in the process of being created, and nothing (except for occasional vocal exhaustion) hinders the composer from ornamenting, adding, and creating continually. When reading a poem that is intended to be oral, the ideology of textuality can make its open "ending" seem forced or unsatisfying to us (Lord 100-101). Thus, the saddest thing about a text is its lack of "next." The reader may have only what the author has chosen to give. On the other side, as much as the author may try to interact with the reader through his writing, he is ultimately inevitably hindered by the very fact of the text. While Eugenides has done his best to surpass the limitations of textuality and bring us a story enriched by oral tradition, in the end he can only invite his eager audience to consider with him what comes "next," and allow his living story to settle down into solid textual residue. Nevertheless, the final words of *Middlesex* are perhaps the most important for our discussion of the novel's hybridity and its relation to gender.

Walter Benjamin, attempting to define the oral storytelling tradition, wrote that "every real story ... contains, openly or covertly, something useful ... less an answer to a question than a proposal concerning the continuation of a story which is just unfolding" (2-3). A defining characteristic of the story is that it has the potential, not only to continue, but to spill into the lives of the listeners and invite them to compose their own variations on its themes. In the case of *Middlesex*, one might say that the "something useful" it contains is its potential—practically an imperative—to continue. The first time that I read the ending of *Middlesex*, I thought that the phrase "what came next" was a reference to Zora's assertion about hermaphrodites: "we're what's next" (490); Cal ends the book thinking about hermaphrodism and intersex rights. But when I read it again, this time with the author's attention to oral tradition in mind, I saw something else in those words: a refusal. Eugenides refuses to give his story an ending. He declines to make concrete what should remain fluid. A novel, particularly one of the *Bildungsroman* genre, is "supposed" to end on a note of finality, beginning with a man's birth and ending with his completion as an adult man. *Middlesex* started with Cal's birth and could easily have ended with his "completion." But in failing—in fact *refusing*—to end the book that way, Eugenides denies that the story of development, of life, and of identity is ever really complete. In contemplating "what comes next," Cal is thinking not only about the physical hermaphrodite, but about the hybrid, fluid, inherently incomplete nature of life in general. As *Middlesex* occupies the space between oral tradition and text, hermpahrodism becomes its symbol for denying dichotomies and embracing in-betweens.

Works Cited

Bahktin, Mikhail. "Discourse in the Novel." *Literary Theory: An Anthology*, 2nd ed., ed. Julie Rivkin and Michael Ryan. Malden, MA: Blackwell Publishing, 2004: 674-685.

Benjamin, Walter. "The Storyteller: Reflections on the Works of Nikolai Leskov." *Illuminations*. Ed. Hannah Arendt, trans. H. Zohn. NY: Schocken Books, 1968.

Butler, Judith. "Performative Acts and Gender Constitution." *Literary Theory: An Anthology*, 2nd ed. Ed. Julie Rivkin and Michael Ryan. Malden, MA: Blackwell Publishing, 2004: 900-911.

Cixous, Helene. "The Laugh of the Medusa." Trans. Keith Cohen and Paula Cohen. Signs 1.4 (1976): 875-893.

Eugenides, Jeffrey. *Middlesex*. New York: Picador, 2002.

Lord, Albert B. *The Singer of Tales*. Cambridge, MA: Harvard University Press, 1960.

Ong, Walter J. *Orality and Literacy: The Technologizing of the Word*. NY: Methuen, 1982.

Smith, William. "Musae." *A Dictionary of Greek and Roman Biography and Mythology*. London: Spottiswoode and Co., 1873. Project Perseus. <http://www.perseus.tufts.edu/hopper/text?doc=Perseus:text:1999.04.0104:entry=musae-bio-1>.

Suffering and the Happiness Movement: What Would Nietzsche Do?

Daniel Michael Murphy
Towson University

> Broadly speaking, a preference for questionable and terrifying things is a symptom of strength; while a taste for the pretty and dainty belongs to the weak and delicate. Pleasure in tragedy characterizes strong ages and natures.... It is the heroic spirits who say Yes to themselves in tragic cruelty: they are hard enough to experience suffering as a pleasure.
> —Friedrich Nietzsche, *The Will to Power*

Introduction

The oldest and most daunting problem of the human condition rests in the feelings of suffering and the conflict of dealing with that suffering. Major religions from Christianity to Buddhism developed out of a focus on the issue of human suffering and how it can be solved. Now contemporary philosophies, following a tradition that suffering is an unnecessary problem of life, suggest a solution through the pursuit of pure happiness and the elimination of suffering. In response, book critics are hailing Eric Wilson, whose work *Against Happiness* plays to the defense of suffering, as the chief opponent against this new happiness movement. However, this debate of happiness versus suffering is far from new, and the best responses go untouched. Both the happiness movement and Eric Wilson fail to utilize the philosophy of Friedrich Nietzsche, who, instead of treating suffering as a

Daniel Murphy graduated from Towson University in 2010 with a major in philosophy and minor in English. He wants to continue interweaving the two disciplines in a Master of Fine Arts program, concentrating on fiction writing.

problem looking for a solution, looks to suffering as a reality, one inseparable from happiness and life itself.

Wilson vs. The Happiness Movement

A specter is haunting America—the specter of happiness. At least it appears so, now that Americans are claiming they are happier than ever. With a new wave of positive thinking and positive psychology, feelings of melancholy and suffering are being sedated by the happiness movement. But the idea that people should only be happy may not be as healthy as is advertised. Wilson's recent book *Against Happiness* attempts to put an end to this happiness addiction by arguing that melancholy inspires great art and feats of the intellect. While Wilson makes a great effort to defend melancholy, he offers little defense of true joy and only tiptoes around the idea of too much suffering.

Wilson's task in *Against Happiness* is to counter "American" happiness with a healthy dose of melancholy. The impetus for Wilson's book is a Pew research poll that states that 85 percent of Americans claim to be happy. Wilson is not convinced this is real happiness. While Wilson focuses on melancholy as it works against happiness, he interchanges various other terms in the mix. At any given point Wilson may speak of the blues, sadness, sorrow, suffering and moderate depression as synonyms for melancholy. For Wilson, happiness and joy are not always identical. But he typically uses "joy" to express what he views as real happiness and not fake American happiness. Wilson rarely clarifies his terminology, except at the book's beginning when he wants to defend his position on melancholy by avoiding confusion with what he calls clinical depression or biochemical disorders:

> There is a fine line between what I'm calling melancholia and what society calls depression. In my mind, what separates the two is degree of activity. Both forms are more or less chronic sadness that leads to ongoing unease with how things are—persistent feelings that the world as it is is not quite right, that it is a place of suffering, stupidity, and evil. Depression (as I see it, at least) causes apathy in the face of the unease, lethargy approaching total paralysis, an inability to feel much of anything one way or another. In contrast, melancholia (in my eyes) generates a deep feeling in regard

to this same anxiety, a turbulence of heart that results in an active questioning of the status quo, a perpetual longing to create new ways of being and seeing. (8)

However, Wilson does not appear to stay true to his stance on depression versus melancholy. Throughout the book, Wilson speaks of the creative genius and great artistic works sparked from periods of tremendous suffering and melancholy, even at times, for men like Beethoven and John Keats, enough to think about suicide. While Wilson often praises this type of melancholy, in his conclusion he states that "Obviously, those suffering severe depression, suicidal and bordering on psychosis, require serious medications. But what of those millions of people who possess mild to moderate depression?" (149). The type of melancholy discussed in the rest of the book does not seem fit under the category of "mild to moderate depression." And Wilson also interchanges the terms melancholy and depression, which he originally set out to clearly separate. Of even greater difficulty is Wilson's concluding statement on melancholy: "melancholia, far from a mere disease or weakness of will, is an almost miraculous invitation to transcend the banal status quo and imagine the untapped possibilities for existence" (145). This seems difficult to place between moderate and severe depression.

Reality through Melancholy

Wilson's attack against positive psychology, the self-help phenomenon, and an overuse of anti-depressant medications is fueled by his argument that melancholy is necessary for a person to experience a real and authentic existence while also offering creative genius. Wilson points out that if Americans would stop pushing the real away, then they could better understand what happiness is: "Forsaking these unrealistic expectations, happy types could for once face the agonized yet ecstatic contraries of life. They could realize that there is no joy without sorrow.... Suddenly sadness would not seem an aberration but instead a vital power, the enabler of joy" (30).

Wilson touches on death as the center to melancholy when he speaks of creative genius: "On the one hand, the melancholy soul hates death, for it causes him endless turmoil and pain. On the other hand, this same melancholy person embraces death because it inspires him to perceive and to create beauty" (131).

The creativity that arises from melancholy can extend from literature, to art, to music and philosophy. Wilson points out excellent examples from history, highlighting not only great works of a melancholic nature but also showing the melancholy the worker went through. People like Herman Melville, Carl Jung, Marsilio Ficino, and John Keats saw that melancholy led to something of great worth, be it creative genius or intellectual insight.

Too Much Suffering?

Wilson offers no examples of the people who decide to take suffering upon themselves in order to achieve wisdom. Aeschylus's notion that "man must suffer to be wise" is not a starting point but a realization one makes afterwards. Ficino spent his life trying to escape suffering before ultimately coming to the understanding that it leads to higher philosophical insight. Wilson points to Beethoven, who experienced terrible melancholy both from his deafness and a gloom already present throughout his life. Beethoven attempted to cure his condition and sought medical advice. Looking to escape his suffering, Beethoven even considered the idea of suicide. However, Beethoven eliminated this possible escape due to the belief of genius still within him, thinking he could not leave the world until he had brought forth his genius (127). It seems clear that these creative geniuses realize that more important than their suffering is their great work. Wilson also points out Keats, who never tried to escape his melancholy. Keats was resigned that he was already a dead man and never tried to escape his fate with religion, drugs, or drinking. Keats took on his melancholy and out of it discovered his belief about suffering: "Do you not see how necessary a World of Pains and troubles is to school an Intelligence and make it a Soul?" (Wilson 110). Wilson points out that Keats was adamant against people falling prey to too much suffering or even to suicide; however, Wilson does not pull at this thread. When Wilson praises the great poetic works of Samuel Taylor Coleridge, he ignores the problem that Coleridge thought his life was meaningless and *worse* than suicide (87). Wilson never examines whether or not Coleridge's suffering was too much—that is, of the type that he warns in his conclusion must be governed by medications. Wilson points to Ernest Hemingway as another innovator of melancholic genius; but he fails to comment on Hemingway's suicide or point out that in Hemingway's most melancholic works (*A Farewell to Arms, For Whom the Bell*

Tolls, Islands of the Stream) the characters experience great suffering to no end. Hemingway's characters, reflective of himself, might indicate examples of too much suffering.

What is Melancholy?

Another difficulty with Wilson's work is his inability to clarify what constitutes the requirements of *his* view of melancholy. Not only does he not get into when a person may have too much melancholy, he does not outline how much melancholy is enough to spark creative genius or what the source of this melancholy may be. While some of the stories, such as those of Beethoven and Keats, show the artists' sources of melancholy as their illness or lifestyles, others like Melville and Ficino are not brought up. Wilson seems to suggest these men just had melancholic moods. Must some serious event of suffering push a person into melancholy? Can a focus on melancholy pull someone deeper into it? The question of what brings melancholy about is not looked into (although in his conclusion, Wilson does suggest a "melancholia gene" within human DNA) (147). Regardless, it is doubtful that just any melancholy would do for Wilson.

Wilson makes a valiant attempt to combat the happiness movement by emphasizing the great creative genius that melancholy can inspire. His history of literary and artistic genius helps show why melancholy should not be negated, but his refusal to tackle the question of too much suffering prevents a deeper look into the real impact of suffering. By ignoring happiness to focus so foolhardily on suffering Wilson makes the same mistake of those in the happiness movement: the radical separation of happiness and suffering.

Introduction to Nietzsche

Nietzsche is the neglected philosopher in this war between the happiness movement and the defenders of suffering. Underlining Nietzsche's doctrine of eternal recurrence and within his notion of *amor fati* is the idea that one must say *Yes* to suffering. For Nietzsche, suffering can be found under two different lights: great and weak. Nietzsche examines the origins of people's understanding of suffering by looking at different cultures. While suffering can turn into a destructive force that feeds the cravings of pity in man and prevents him from succeeding in the process of overcoming, suffering must not be neglected. Suffering, like joy, is part of life and must be understood as such.

Great Versus Weak Suffering

Nietzsche himself does not specifically distinguish what we can understand as his two main concepts of suffering: great suffering and weak suffering. On the surface, great suffering connotes a positive reflection from Nietzsche while weak suffering connotes the opposite. Great suffering is that which is closest to the Dionysian, to the great artists, those who suffer to be wise, and above all those who overcome and endure suffering. Weak suffering constitutes sickness and those bodies that are weakened, as well as those whose suffering differs from the great sufferers. Weak sufferers might follow the ascetic ideal, thus explaining their sickliness. Christians also make up the weak sufferers and the support of them.

Romantic sufferers might appear to fall under their own category, but what is important is separating them from the great Dionysian sufferers. In *The Gay Science*, Nietzsche divides non-weak sufferers under two categories: those suffering from the over-fullness of life and those suffering from the impoverishment of life (Sec. 370). The former are the great or Dionysian sufferers who have Nietzsche's support. The latter are the romantics who seek an escape from suffering not by overcoming it but by being relieved of it. The romantics might have a taste for the tragic, but ultimately they wish to escape it. While the romantics do not fall directly in line with the weak sufferers—for Nietzsche might see that they still hold some worth with their ideas and artistic efforts that the weak sufferers do not have—they must be kept separate from the great sufferers.

Greeks and Tragedy

An examination of Nietzsche's view on suffering begins with his understanding of tragedy and the Greeks. Here Nietzsche looks to compare the two Greek spirits, Apollo and Dionysus (spirits in a cultural, not a metaphysical, sense). The Apollonian spirit, based on the god Apollo, is referential to the individual, and that which is structured, while the Dionysian, based on Dionysus, tears down the walls of individuation by using a dash of madness.

Silenus, the mythological satyr and mascot of the Dionysian spirit, turns the Greek world upside down with his wise words: "Oh, wretched ephemeral race, children of chance and misery, why do you compel me to tell you what it would be most expedient for you not to hear? What is best of all is utterly beyond your reach: not to be born, not to *be*, to be *nothing*. But the second best for you is—to die soon" (*Tragedy* Sec. 3). The Greeks, however, do not cave in to the thought of death, but embrace it with their great art—the tragedy.

It was the Greeks, as exemplified by Aeschylus's statement, "suffer to be wise," that invented the art of tragedy. For Nietzsche, the Greeks overcame suffering to produce from their wisdom great artistic works (*Tragedy* Sec. 3). The Apollonian desire to overcome meets with the Dionysian truth of life, and the two spirits together give rise to the great art of tragedy. Rather than succumb to suffering, the Greeks implement it as a necessary part of existence. The wisest men, the heroes of tragedy, are forced through their wisdom to experience great suffering. One can see the "suffer to be wise" motto also as "if wise, then suffer." Nietzsche cites both Oedipus and Prometheus as two figures who, to gain wisdom, were dealt a punishment of suffering. Nietzsche describes Oedipus:

> the most sorrowful figure of the Greek stage, the unfortunate Oedipus, as the noble human being who, in spite of his wisdom, is destined to error and misery but who eventually, through his tremendous suffering, spreads a magical power of blessing that remains effective even beyond his decease. (*Tragedy* Sec. 9)

Nietzsche goes on to describe Aeschylus's Prometheus:

> In himself the Titanic artist found the defiant faith that he had the ability to create men and at least destroy Olympian gods, by means of his superior wisdom which, to be sure, he had to atone for with eternal suffering. The splendid "ability" of the great genius for which even eternal suffering is a slight price, the stern pride of the *artist*. (*Tragedy* Sec. 9)

Tragic heroes take action and pay the price, as opposed to the chorus, which stands in the shadows unwilling to act. The individual heroes are the sufferers, not the masses of the chorus.

Nietzsche unveils the origin of suffering in connection with man existing as an individual. Nietzsche explains that with Dionysian suffering, "we are therefore to regard the state of individuation as the origin and primal cause of all suffering" (*Tragedy* Sec. 10). With the Apollonian view, one as an individual sees his individuality separate from the totality. However, the Dionysian spirit teaches that the individual is still part of that totality. Nietzsche explains how Apollo adapts to the Dionysian wisdom: "he shows us how necessary is the entire world of suffering, that by means of it the individual may be impelled to realize the redeeming vision, and then, sunk in contemplation of it, sit quietly in his tossing bark, amid the waves" (*Tragedy* Sec. 4). Man suffers individually but should overcome that suffering by realizing the totality and seeing himself as part of that totality. Suffering, therefore, is not an evil of life, but a line of wisdom that breaks the gap between the individual and the world.

Is Suffering Good?

Artists can wield the tool of suffering like an inspirational muse. Nietzsche writes: "Art as the *redemption of the sufferer*—as the way to states in which suffering is willed, transfigured, deified, where suffering is a form of great delight" (*Will* Sec. 853). Nietzsche points out two Germans, Schiller and Goethe, who correctly identify the role of Greek tragedy and incorporate it in their poetry (*Tragedy* Sec. 7).

Nietzsche's embrace of suffering goes beyond its role in tragedy. One need look no further than *Beyond Good and Evil* to witness whether or not Nietzsche approves of suffering:

> You want, if possible—and there is no more insane "if possible"—*to abolish suffering*. And we? It really seems that *we* would rather have it higher and worse than ever. Well-being as you understand it—that is no goal, that seems to us an *end*, a state that soon makes man ridiculous and contemptible—that makes his destruction *desirable*. The discipline of suffering, of *great* suffering—do you not know that only this discipline has created all enhancements of man so far? That tension of the soul in unhappiness which cultivates its

> strength, its shudders face to face with great ruin, its inventiveness and courage in enduring, persevering, interpreting, and exploiting suffering, and whatever has been granted to it of profundity, secret, mask, spirit, cunning, greatness—was it not granted to it through suffering, through the discipline of great suffering? (*Beyond* Sec. 225)

For artists, suffering can be requisite, and their creation is the great redemption from suffering. In *Thus Spoke Zarathustra*, Nietzsche's prophet, Zarathustra, speaks of the possibility of creating *great* works (Sec. "Upon the Blessed Isles"). The pain of suffering, when overcome, can be redeemed with great creation.

Nietzsche himself offers the proof of the accomplishments man makes from overcoming suffering. Nietzsche was quite physically ill and suffered from his failure to succeed in life. His social life was stricken with friends turning into enemies and a lack of family. But Nietzsche thrived from this. In *Ecce Homo*, as Kaufmann points out, are found Nietzsche's thoughts on his own illness just a few weeks prior to collapsing (Sec. "Human, All-Too-Human" 4). Here Nietzsche praises his sickness:

> Sickness *detached me slowly*: it spared me any break, any violent and offensive step. Thus I did not lose any good will and actually gained not a little. My sickness also gave me the right to change all my habits completely; it permitted, it *commanded* me to forget; it bestowed on me the necessity of lying still, of leisure, of waiting and being patient.— But that means, of thinking.— My eyes alone put an end to all bookwormishness—in brief, philology: I was delivered from the "book"; for years I did not read a thing—the greatest benefit I ever conferred on myself.—That nethermost self which had, as it were, been buried and grown silent under the continual pressure of having to listen to other selves (and that is after all what reading means) awakened slowly, shyly, dubiously—but eventually it spoke again. Never have I felt happier with myself than in the sickest and most painful periods of my life: one only need look at *The Dawn* or perhaps *The Wanderer and His Shadow* to comprehend what this 'return to myself' meant—a supreme kind of recovery.

— The other kind merely followed from this. (Sec. "Human, All-Too-Human" 4)

Nietzsche's appreciation for the physical problems of his eyesight, which prevented him from reading, shows his mentality is that of *amor fati*. His suffering was capable of leading him exactly where he needed to go, a "supreme kind of recovery." Nietzsche says *Yes* to suffering not only out of *amor fati* but also from the wisdom suffering imparts.

The concept of *amor fati* is the pinnacle of being human, in Nietzsche's eyes. His doctrine of the eternal recurrence of the same, of saying *Yes* to living the same life over and over again, thrives on *amor fati*. Nietzsche writes: "My formula for greatness in a human being is *amor fati*: that one wants nothing to be different, not forward, not backward, not in all eternity. Not merely bear what is necessary, still less conceal it… but *love* it" (*Ecce* Sec. "Why Am I So Clever" 10).

But Nietzsche's own suffering, just as that of the other great artists he described, was endured and overcome. Great suffering, in relation to Nietzsche's category, requires *endurance*. While many would want to know the advantages of suffering, for Nietzsche, suffering is not something that produces either good or evil; instead, suffering is a necessary part of life that can either be endured or not. Suffering becomes a test of endurance. Nietzsche writes: "I assess the power of a will by how much resistance, pain, torture it endures and knows how to turn to its advantage; I do not account the evil and painful character of existence a reproach to it, but hope rather that it will one day be more evil and painful than hitherto" (*Will* Sec. 382). Nietzsche continues his thoughts on endurance in the end of his notes in *The Will to Power* when he addresses his possible disciples:

> To those human beings who are of any concern to me I wish suffering, desolation, sickness, ill-treatment, indignities—I wish that they should not remain unfamiliar with profound self-contempt, the torture of self-mistrust, the wretchedness of the vanquished: I have no pity for them, because I wish them the only thing that can prove today whether one is worth anything or not—that one endures. (Sec. 910)

Nietzsche on Pity

Endurance is for the great sufferers, not the weak. The weak sufferers are those that not only do not overcome, but do not want to overcome suffering. These sufferers are of the variety that either chooses suffering as in the ascetic ideal or wishes their sickness to vanish. Nietzsche uses this view of suffering to look into the origins of guilt and cruelty. Nietzsche expounds that it was the act of cruelty, of imparting suffering onto others or bearing witness of others' suffering, that gave rise to guilt. In *On the Genealogy of Morals,* Nietzsche accounts for this origin. The sufferer does something for the observer of suffering, feeding the cruel nature of man. The desire to inflict suffering is part of this nature: "To see others suffer does one good, to make others suffer even more: this is a hard saying but an ancient, mighty, human, all-too-human principle.... Without cruelty there is no festival: thus the longest and most ancient part of human history teaches—and in punishment there is so much that is *festive!*" (*Genealogy* Essay 2 Sec. 6). Nietzsche's depiction of earlier ages, where man desires to see others suffer in order to benefit from the pleasure of the festival of cruelty, differs from what arises in the form of pity.

There was a reversal where the spectacle of suffering needed to be explained, for the idea of senseless suffering was too much. Nietzsche suggests that man had to do whatever it took to deny the idea of senseless suffering, ranging from the Christian invention of salvation to the ancients' understanding of a great spectator (*Genealogy* Essay 2 Sec. 7). This explanation of suffering departs from earlier times when cruelty was acceptable. Nietzsche declares:

> Today, when suffering is always brought forward as the principal argument *against* existence, as the worst question mark, one does well to recall the ages in which the opposite opinion prevailed because men were unwilling to refrain from *making* suffering and saw in it an enchantment of the first order, a genuine seduction *to* life. (*Genealogy* Essay 2 Sec. 7)

The view of suffering as an argument against existence is one Nietzsche sees as both false and a notion that for a long time was never even considered. When suffering became understood to be so terrible as to argue against the existence of life, feelings about witnessing suffering changed as well. Instead of taking pleasure in the festival of cruelty, people felt pity.

In regard to weak suffering, it might be pity that Nietzsche is most against. In tragedy it was shown how the individual in suffering learns of the totality. The connection between individuation and suffering was crucial. However, pity works against the personal level of suffering. Nietzsche explains:

> Our personal and profoundest suffering is incomprehensible and inaccessible to almost everyone.... But whenever people *notice* that we suffer, they interpret our suffering superficially. It is the very essence of the emotion of pity that it strips away from the suffering of others whatever is distinctively personal. (*The Gay Science* Sec. 338)

Pity removes the individuation of suffering by having others attempt to share in an individual's suffering. They might liken their own experiences to the situation of the sufferer, proclaiming how they have been through it and know how it feels. But pity is a failed attempt at sharing suffering, which Nietzsche proclaims should not be sought: "I want to teach them what is understood by so few today, least of all by these preachers of pity: *to share not suffering but joy*" (*The Gay Science* Sec. 338). It is joy, not suffering, which is to be shared. The intoxication of laughter spreads among people, for joy represents the totality, the Dionysian. However, the tears of one are not felt by the other as real suffering, but only as pity or compassion. But this is not a problem for Nietzsche, for suffering is and should remain personal and individual.

If pity is a false path, the question becomes: what can one do when someone is suffering? Since suffering cannot be shared, nor passed off like a burden, the answer lies in the opposite direction: joy. What man can do for fellow man is share in joy. Zarathustra declares: "Verily, I may have done this and that for sufferers; but always I seemed to have done better when I learned to feel better joys. As long as there have been men, man has felt too little joy: that alone, my brothers, is our original sin. And learning better to feel joy, we learn best to not hurt others or to plan hurts for them" (*Zarathustra* Sec. "On the Pitying"). And for those already suffering, they should mostly be left to their privacy, for they must endure their own suffering. Instead of offering pity, Zarathustra offers a field cot: "But if you have a suffering friend, be a resting place for his suffering, but a hard bed as it were, a field cot: thus you will profit him best" (ibid).

Nietzsche on the Sick, the Christians, and the Ascetic Ideal

More detrimental to man than pity is the weak suffering proposed by Christians and ascetics. They have excluded suffering from being part of the experience or knowledge of life, and into a representation of virtue. These types of weak sufferers are more than glad to experience suffering. They represent sickness to suggest to the healthy that something is wrong with this gap between healthy and sick. The weak sufferers play a superior role, making the strong feel guilty. Nietzsche points out this terrible possibility: "Undoubtedly if they succeeded in *poisoning the consciences* of the fortunate with their own misery, with all misery, so that one day the fortunate began to be ashamed of their good fortune and perhaps said one to another: 'it is disgraceful to be fortunate: *there is too much misery!*'" (*Genealogy* Essay 3 Sec. 14). Nietzsche sees that this attempt to make the fortunate feel ashamed of their good fortune because of others' misery will be terrible for man. One of the worst possibilities is for the sick to infect the healthy, replacing strength and endurance with sickness as the new symbol of virtue.

Nietzsche looks upon the ascetics as those that ask, "why do I suffer?" Weak sufferers want to identify the cause behind their suffering before even examining its true nature. Nietzsche writes:

> For every sufferer instinctively seeks a cause for his suffering; more exactly, an agent; still more specifically, a *guilty* agent who is susceptible to suffering—in short, some living thing upon which he can, on some pretext or other, vent his affects, actually or in effigy: for the venting of his affects represents the greatest attempt on the part of the suffering to win relief, *anaesthesia*—the narcotic he cannot help desiring to deaden pain of any kind.... "Someone or other must be to blame for my feeling ill"—this kind of reasoning is common to all the sick. (*Genealogy* Essay 3 Sec. 15)

But the question, "Why do I suffer?" leads people in the wrong direction. This question implies that one should not suffer at all—that is, that suffering is bad. It also suggests that there may be an outside cause for suffering such as gods who might look upon and compare those who are fortunate to those in suffering. Finally, this question, "Why do I suffer?" separates the individual from the totality.

Christianity herds these weak sufferers together to help them answer this question. Nietzsche describes Christianity: "As religion of sin (of transgression against God as the only kind of transgression, as the sole cause of suffering in general), with a universal cure for it" (*The Will to Power* Sec. 181). Sin is revealed as the cause of suffering. And easily enough, an antidote is presented in the concept of salvation. This alleviates the sickness these weak sufferers feel.

Nietzsche is not Against Happiness

Presented with Nietzsche's views on great and weak suffering, it is important to note that Nietzsche is not against happiness. Few philosophers are as life-affirming as Nietzsche. Happiness, alongside suffering, is included in the affirmation of life. When one says yes to life, to living it over and over again, one emphatically says yes to all happiness and joy. But with Nietzsche's thoughts on suffering in hand, we can understand how he does not strive merely for just happiness.

As Zarathustra proclaims at the end of *Thus Spoke Zarathustra*, it is not happiness or suffering he is concerned with but the umbrella above them both: "My suffering and my pity for suffering—what does it matter? Am I concerned with *happiness*? I am concerned with my *work*" (Sec. "The Sign").

Suffering and happiness come together in life. If one were to only seek happiness, he would betray the true nature of life, and fail to experience true joy. Nietzsche details the danger of only wanting happiness:

> If you refuse to let your own suffering lie upon you even for an hour and if you constantly try to prevent and forestall all possible distress way ahead of time; if you experience suffering and displeasure as evil, hateful, worthy of annihilation, and as a defect of existence, then it is clear that besides your religion of pity you also harbor another religion in your heart that is perhaps the mother of the religion of pity: the religion of comfortableness. How little you know of human happiness, you comfortable and benevolent people, for

happiness and unhappiness are sisters and even twins that either grow up together or, as in your case, remain small together. (*The Gay Science* Sec. 338)

The twin sisters of happiness and suffering are both necessary experiences of life that make up its real nature. Nietzsche addresses those who desire a true world, which appears to be a world of only happiness:

Man seeks "the truth": a world that is not self-contradictory, not deceptive, does not change, a *true* world—a world in which one does not suffer; contradiction, deception, change—causes of suffering! He does not doubt that a world as it ought to be exists; he would like to seek out the road to it.... Whence does man here derive the concept *reality*? — Why is it that he derives *suffering* from change, deception, contradiction? And why not rather his happiness? (*The Will to Power*)

Joy in its highest faculty, that true moment of joy that for Nietzsche affirms the existence of life and says *Yes* to living it over and over again, may be desired for eternity (*Zarathustra* Sec. "The Drunken Song"). But woe and suffering comes with it. Man may want the suffering to go away but will want it to return once more. Zarathustra proclaims: "Have you ever said Yes to a single joy? O my friends, then you said Yes too to *all* woe. All things are entangled, ensnared, enamored; if ever you wanted one thing twice, if ever you said, 'You please me, happiness! Abide, moment!' then you wanted *all* back. All anew, all eternally, all entangled, ensnared, enamored—oh, then you *loved* the world. Eternal ones, love it eternally and evermore; and to woe too, you say: go, but return! *For all joy wants—eternity*" (ibid.).

Wilson and Nietzsche

Nietzsche would step right in with Wilson to combat the happiness movement. The overly optimistic optimists who peddle positive thoughts harder than depression drugs might even be worse for mankind than the weak sufferers. But Wilson's approach to this issue is like the happiness movement in that both are aiming towards a single goal, albeit in opposite directions. To do so in either case, as Nietzsche shows, would betray the true nature of life. One must not choose either happiness or suffering, viewing them as separate goals. Nietzsche expresses that one must simply live, accepting and loving the happiness and the suffering that befalls one's fate.

Works Cited

Wilson, Eric. *Against Happiness*. NY: Sarah Crichton Books, 2009.

Nietzsche, Friedrich. *Beyond Good and Evil*. Trans. Walter Kaufmann. NY: Modern Library, 2000.

———. *The Birth of Tragedy*. Trans. Walter Kaufmann. NY: Modern Library, 2000.

———. *Ecce Homo*. Trans. Walter Kaufmann. NY: Modern Library, 2000.

———. *The Gay Science*. Trans. Walter Kaufmann. NY: Vintage, 1974.

———. *On the Genealogy of Morals*. Trans. Walter Kaufmann. NY: Modern Library, 2000.

———. *Thus Spoke Zarathustra*. Trans. Walter Kaufmann. NY: Penguin Books, 1982.

———. *The Will to Power*. Trans. Walter Kaufmann. NY: Vintage, 1968.

Hopkins Goes to War:
The Saga of the 18th General Hospital

Fletcher Boone
The Johns Hopkins University

Introduction

In the years immediately preceding America's entrance into World War II, the U.S. government ordered prominent teaching hospitals to prepare members of their staffs for deployment overseas to care for wounded soldiers. One such institution was the Johns Hopkins University Hospital, which was asked to supply enough men and women to staff two complete field hospitals. Nearly two hundred Johns Hopkins doctors, nurses, and other medical professionals quickly volunteered, forming the 18th and 118th General Hospitals of the U.S. Army Medical Service Corps. After the Pearl Harbor attack in December 1941, both units were sent to the Pacific theater with only rudimentary military training. Once there, the 18th and 118th served overseas for almost three years, providing critical care to thousands of uniformed men and women.

This paper will attempt to assess what the wartime experience was like for the members of the 18th General Hospital by considering the perspectives revealed in three different primary source bases. The paper will begin with an introduction to the 18th General Hospital, spanning from its inception in 1941 to its deactivation in 1945. It will then discuss the memoir *L.O.D.—Yes*, a factually

Fletcher Boone is currently a senior at The Johns Hopkins University, majoring in history and psychology. He wants to attend graduate school in one of those fields. Until he decides, he is considering intelligence work, foreign service or journalism.

complete history of the 18th. Then the paper will examine *The Fijitive*, the newspaper published by the 18th for internal consumption. Created for entertainment purposes, it offers a lighthearted yet informative take on the unit's tenure in the Pacific. In addition to detailing what the unit's members did during their considerable free time, the newspaper clues the reader into the 18th's emotional state. Next, a close look at letters from one member of the 18th will reveal a unique perspective, one that is able to fill in considerable gaps in the historical narrative left by the other sources. The paper will conclude by attempting to determine the legacy of the unit's experience during World War II. In doing so, the paper will answer the following questions. Did members of the 18th General Hospital view their experience as a disappointment? Were their lofty expectations regarding the nature of their service met? Finally, is the generally negative portrayal of the 18th's experience in both primary and secondary sources justified?

Of the three source bases discussed in the paper, only the memoir is used in secondary literature in any capacity. Both *The Fijitive* and the letters are completely absent from secondary accounts of the Hopkins medical unit. By examining the perspectives offered in these two "new" sources, we may achieve a fuller picture of the 18th General Hospital's experience during its overseas odyssey in World War II.

The 18th's War

The Second World War officially began in September of 1939, when Nazi forces invaded Poland. This unprovoked attack triggered the bloodiest war in human history and put the United States on a collision course with the Axis powers. Back in Baltimore, however, the Johns Hopkins Hospital and Medical School were largely untouched by the opening of hostilities. In his history of the two institutions, however, historian Thomas Turner writes that they soon "began to stir; energies and thoughts began gradually to be diverted from teaching and research and to be fixed on some problem believed important to the war effort" (471). More tangible signs of Hopkins's involvement could be seen in the winter of 1939-1940. Hopkins employees in the Army and Navy reserves were pressed into active duty and entire laboratories in the medical school were appropriated by the military for war-related research (Turner 472).

In early 1940 it became clear that Johns Hopkins would become directly involved in the war effort if America did in fact enter the conflict. In March, the Army Surgeon General asked Johns Hopkins Hospital to ready a portion of its staff for deployment overseas. Several weeks later, the Army informed Hopkins that it would need to part with nearly two hundred doctors and nurses to staff not one, but two entire general hospitals. According to Mary Condon-Rall and Albert Cowdrey, authors of a history of the military's medical services in the Pacific theater, such hospitals were the largest and most valuable in military service, often containing the best medical professionals available. General hospitals were typically located many miles from the front lines and tasked to "provide comprehensive care for severe cases throughout a theatre of war" (71). The Army designated the two Johns Hopkins units the 18th and 118th General Hospitals respectively, the former's unit number meant to pay homage to the Johns Hopkins medical unit that served during World War I (Turner 472). But without a formal declaration of war on the part of the U.S. government, the 18th existed only on paper, and life at Hopkins returned to normal for the next several months (Turner 483).

The Pearl Harbor attacks of December 7, 1941 brought this period of relative calm to an abrupt end. Both Hopkins units were activated soon after America's entrance into the war, and their constituents ordered to report for active duty. On April 20, 1942, the forty-five doctors and sixty nurses of the 18th left Baltimore's Pennsylvania Station, heading by train south to Fort Jackson, South Carolina. There the Army, according to Turner, attempted to "make soldiers of these civilian physicians and nurses" but only achieved "limited success" (484). At Fort Jackson, the unit learned the basics of military discipline and secrecy. Each member also had to fill out of reams of paperwork, or as one of the 18th's officers remembered it, the "repetitious filling out of multitudinous blanks" (Tilghman 4). After two weeks in South Carolina, the 18th was shipped to San Francisco, California. From this the unit inferred that it was heading to the Pacific theater, but the Army did not reveal its exact destination. In late May 1942, the 18th General Hospital boarded the *U.S.S. General James Parker* and headed west across the Pacific Ocean (ibid).

The 18th General Hospital, along with a division of Marines, landed on the island of Fiji on August 3, 1942. Instead of quickly becoming operational, the unit was beset by problems from the very start. First, the Army had not assigned the unit a location to set up a hospital. After days of "excruciating delay," the 18th's commanding officer chose an unassuming site: the athletic field of a local boarding school (Tilghman 5). Second, the medical equipment needed for the hospital to function had not yet arrived, and would not arrive for an additional three weeks. In the meantime, the members of the 18th, along with a unit of Army Engineers, began enthusiastically constructing the hospital's first facilities. According to Colonel Carmichael Tilghman, one of the unit's doctors, the 18th's members "engaged in this endeavor so aptly that they were known as the '18th General Engineers'" (10). Nevertheless, the 18th General Hospital was unable to receive patients until October 1942, nearly five months after leaving San Francisco. This lengthy delay grated on the unit's members, who were frustrated that their professional skills went unutilized for so long.

The initial patients the hospital received were battle casualties from the Guadalcanal campaign. While the nurses and doctors cared for them, Army Engineers and other members of the 18th rapidly expanded the hospital's facilities. Colonel Tilghman writes, "ward tents were pitched while cement was being poured for the floors," and "the doors and windows were installed only after the patients had been admitted" (14-16). Even in the surgery ward, "the carpenters hammered and the surgeons operated side by side."[1] By the end of 1942, the hospital had running water, adequate electricity, and cement walkways and floors, all essentially provided by the unit's own efforts. One of the unit's nurses, Elizabeth McLaughlin, wrote: "Those [cement] walks are tread upon reverently, for we have watched and done the pouring of every square."[2] After several more months of work, the hospital became "Fiji's Hopkins."[3] By mid 1943, it was a sophisticated and self-sustaining installation, complete with a surgery ward and X-ray machines.

Through the first half of 1943, the 18th General Hospital continued to receive many patients. During this time, the hospital tended to an average of seven hundred patients at once, and the census even peaked at a thousand, quite a load for a five-hundred-bed hospital. During this period usually every bed was filled and many ambulatory patients were housed off-site, either in tents or native-style *bure* huts. The great skill of the Hopkins doctors and nurses was readily apparent, as only eleven patients died during the hospital's first year of operation. However, only a small portion of these admitted patients were battle casualties, due to the fact that the nearly uninterrupted stream of American victories had pushed the front lines further and further away from Fiji. Consequently, most of the patients suffered from relatively mild and pedestrian ailments such as jaundice, fungal infections, and ruptured eardrums, a fact that was quite frustrating for the highly skilled Hopkins doctors. According to Colonel Tilghman, much of his professional work in Fiji was "never very inspiring" (Tilghman 25).

The patient census dropped dramatically beginning in late 1943, due to Fiji's increasing unimportance in the war effort. During the final six months of the unit's stay in Fiji, the average patient census was just over a hundred, and battle casualties were no longer brought to Fiji. Due to the lack of professional work, the 18th undertook extensive measures to combat boredom. In 1943 the unit, with the help of Army Engineers, built a five-hundred–seat amphitheatre. Called the Kava Bowl, the amphitheatre was host to daily events. Movies shown three times a week were "enthusiastically patronized" by both members of the 18th and its patients, and musical performances by unit members and natives drew large crowds.[4] The 18th also partook heavily in athletics, forming basketball, football, baseball, softball, and volleyball teams. The 18th also began publishing its own newspaper, *The Fijitive*, and held a full-fledged "County Fair and Field Day" twice during its stay in Fiji. But even these could only do so much. Tilghman states that the "monotony of the tropics combined with enforced idleness, after two years of foreign service, became increasingly difficult to endure" (27).

In June, 1944, the Army, recognizing that the 18th General Hospital was woefully underutilized in Fiji, decided to redeploy the unit to the India-Burma theatre. On September 16th, 1944, the unit left Fiji, accompanied by mixed feelings. Some did not like being moved further from home, but others were hopeful that the "professional skill and ability of the Hospital Staff might be utilized to the fullest after all" (Tilghman 28). This was not to be, however. The unit arrived in Bombay, India, and promptly boarded trains heading to Assam. After a weeklong trip on "uniformly antiquated, dirty and uncomfortable" trains, the unit reached their station in Ledo, Assam (Tilghman 31). To the unit's dismay, they found that two other general hospitals were already operating in the area, and "no plan for the [18th's] use had been evolved" (Tilghman 32) by the Army. Even so, the 18th was ordered to construct basic facilities and to prepare to receive casualties. The members of the unit did just that, but they saw very few patients. According to Tilghman, "the professional activity of the 18th General Hospital had reached a low level of stagnation" (35). The unit continued in this state for several months, until it was notified by the Army that all Hopkins-affiliated members of the unit were being rotated back to the United States. On March 22, 1945, the Johns Hopkins doctors and nurses departed their hospital in India-Burma, beginning their journey home. From this point onward, the 18th General Hospital ceased to be a Johns Hopkins-affiliated outfit (Tilghman 39).

The Official Take

The most complete account of the overseas experience of the 18th General Hospital is *L.O.D.—Yes: an Odyssey of the Army's 18th General Hospital*. Written by Richard Carmichael Tilghman, one of the 18th's doctors and its official historian, *L.O.D.—Yes* (*L.O.D.* standing for "line of duty") was intended to be the definitive work chronicling the 18th General Hospital. In the memoir's preface, Tilghman writes, "primarily it was written as a memoir for members of the outfit, secondarily for others that they may have some conception of the environment and the three years overseas service in World War II" (Preface). Published in 1949, Tilghman's memoir is the only memoir of the 18th General Hospital known to exist and is by far the most factually complete source concerning the unit, precisely chronicling its travels and exploits.

Lieutenant Colonel Richard Carmichael Tilghman was a man of many titles. He was a one of the unit's ranking medical officers ("doctors," in military parlance), serving as its Chief of Medicine and Executive Officer of the Hospital (Ross). As mentioned above, he was also appointed by those in the unit as the 18th's official historian. As such, Tilghman took dozens of photographs and shot over two hours of film, in addition to writing and publishing *L.O.D.—Yes*. But what made him beloved to many in the unit was his love of a good time (Ross). He served at the 18th's Special Service Officer, which meant that it was his duty to keep morale up by providing the unit with entertainment. He organized numerous concerts, movie-viewings, and USO shows.[5] He was the driving force behind the two County Fair and Field Days, which others in the unit regarded with particular fondness ("Tattler" 3). The naming of the streets of the 18th's facility in Fiji after prominent Baltimore thoroughfares such as Charles Street and Broadway was his idea.[6] Likewise, it was Tilghman's idea to bring to Fiji the Toad Derby, a time-honored Johns Hopkins tradition in which participants raced wild toads for sometimes considerable amounts of money ("Tattler" 3).

In *L.O.D.—Yes*, Tilghman expounds the history of the 18th General Hospital in painstaking detail, beginning with the events that led to its creation in 1940 and ending with the rotation home of the unit's last Johns Hopkins members. The author never fails to use exact dates, to list the full name and rank of every person mentioned, and to include the proper names of every country, region, city, town or even village that the unit stayed in, passed through, or visited. Tilghman even manages to include the designations of every other unit the 18th encountered and stated names of every ship the 18th either rode in or was escorted by. For example, this is how Tilghman describes the 18th's departure from San Francisco Bay in May of 1942:

> On Sunday, May 24, 1942, the 18th General Hospital (45 officers, 60 nurses, 275 enlisted men, and 7 Red Cross workers, dietitians, and physical therapists) was among the 2000 troops embarking on the U.S. Army Transport, The General James Parker, recently converted 14,000 ton luxury liner, the S.S. Panama. In convoy with The Parker were The President Coolidge, The President Monroe, The General Tasker H. Bliss, The Uruguay, The Santa Clara and The Santa Lucia, bearing the entire Task Force 6429. Escorted by one destroyer and one heavy cruiser, The San Francisco, the convoy passed through the Golden Gate at 1330 hours, 26 May 1942. (4)

This degree of specificity is unparalleled. No other source comes remotely close in *L.O.D.—Yes* in this regard, likely explaining why it has been the sole source used in the secondary literature on the subject.

A striking example of Tilghman's obsessive attention to detail is when he describes the common diseases and injuries treated by the 18th's medical staff during the war. As befitting a doctor, he spends a considerable amount of space enumerating these ailments, filling nearly four pages doing so. It may not seem possible, but here he went into even further detail, bringing his considerable medical knowledge to bear on the subject. To illustrate, here is an excerpt from Tilghman's evaluation of the condition of a group of Marines wounded in the Guadalcanal campaign:

> Uniformly there was malnutrition, many having lost as much as forty pounds in weight. Malaria, jaundice and psychoneuroses were

the outstanding medical conditions necessitating evacuation of the patient from the combat area. Many blast injuries and compound fractures were present. Noteworthy were the severe comminuted fractures of the calcaneous [heel bone], sustained by seamen standing on deck when their ship was torpedoed under them. The acute psychoneurotic evacuee imposed one of the most difficult problems. (19)

Tilghman's *L.O.D.—Yes* is a supremely detailed source, providing just about every objective fact one would like to know about the 18th General Hospital. The author may have treated his subject matter too objectively, however; the surprising lack of emotional content leaves Tilghman's prose feeling rather sterile and uninspired. In short, *L.O.D.—Yes* is a factually illuminating, yet somewhat superficial account of the wartime experience of the 18th General Hospital.

The Fijitive

Starting in early 1944, The 18th General Hospital began publishing *The Fijitive*, the unit's own internal newspaper. Subtitled "Escape From Boredom," *The Fijitive* was created in order to keep the unit busier and to improve morale. The newspaper was published weekly and featured highly entertaining and often humorous reporting. To outsiders, however, *The Fijitive* provides more than entertainment; it offers the reader substantial insight into the thoughts, feelings, and daily life of the 18th General Hospital.

The Fijitive was the brainchild of Sergeant Abe Abramowitz, one of the 18th's enlisted men and a veritable Renaissance man. Proficient at playing both the bass cello and the fiddle, the chaplain's assistant also organized a charitable foundation for Fijian boys and acted as the unit's rabbi. In early 1944, Sergeant Abramowitz decided to do something about the sagging morale of his unit. With the approval of the 18th's commanding officer, Colonel George Finney, Abramowitz began working on a newspaper for the outfit. The Sergeant recruited several other members of the 18th and his project soon became *The Fijitive*.[7]

Abramowitz and his ad hoc staff published *The Fijitive*'s first issue on March 26th, 1944. Although quite brief at only two pages long, subsequent issues soon doubled, and then tripled, in length as the newspaper's scope and popularity grew. The first issue featured extensive coverage of the 18th's sports matches (against other units on Fiji), local entertainment listings, and "The Tattler," the newspaper's gossip column. *The Fijitive*'s staff quickly expanded the newspaper to include editorials, letters to the editor, and comic accounts of notable events from the unit's tenure in the Pacific. Its contributors also weighed in on more serious topics, such as news of the war's progress and significant developments back home. After a successful six-month run, publication of *The Fijitive* ceased in September, 1944, just before the unit redeployed to the India-Burma theater.

The mission of *The Fijitive* was twofold. According to Colonel Richard Graham in the first issue, the 18th created the publication in order to meld the 18th General Hospital into a more cohesive outfit by "bringing to the attention of all, informal and personal news items of interest" (1). The 18th's officers felt that a unit newspaper would strengthen the bonds between the medical officers, nurses, and enlisted men so that they could all better perform their duties. Although not explicitly stated by Col. Graham, *The Fijitive* had another reason for existing. As indicated by its subtitle, "Escape From Boredom," it was also created to boost the *esprit de corps* at a time when it was particularly low. According to Daphine Doster, one of the unit's nurses, "One way to keep busy and keep morale high was to publish our own paper—*The Fijitive*." The editors and contributors of the periodical achieved this end by using humor to great effect and gearing the reporting towards entertaining subjects, such as athletics and gossip.

During *The Fijitive*'s six-month publication, the 18th General Hospital admitted very few patients, so its constituents generally had very little to do. The 18th's newspaper serves as a record of the myriad activities unit members partook in order to fill their excessive free time. These activities included playing sports, attending movies, concerts, and dances, throwing fairs and carnivals, and taking trips to the beach. Many members of the 18th elected to use their time a little more productively, taking courses and lessons in everything from trigonometry to ballroom dancing. The breadth of these activities and the gusto with which they were undertaken were astounding. By revealing how members of the unit spent their idle moments, a subject conspicuously absent from Tilghman's *L.O.D.—Yes*, *The Fijitive* can help outsiders better understand the true nature of their wartime experience.

The Fijitive also provides outsiders with insight into the trappings of life in uniform. For example, the July 6th edition includes an article concerning the ramifications of the recently passed G.I. Bill, and the August 31st issue contains a notice listing the possible punishments for being caught out and about after curfew. Also, the "A Letter to the Editors" section was home to persistent complaints about the lack of both mail and furloughs home. Even more enlightening are the brief memoirs submitted to the paper by unit members. Much about military life can be learned from these accounts, which almost universally described horrendous experiences (usually for comic effect). For example, in the May 26th edition, Sergeant M. Kehoe described his "greatest" memory of the war: being shipped across the Pacific Ocean in a hideously overcrowded vessel. The Sgt. amusingly recounts the ghastly experience where "intimacy was the keynote" (4).

More significantly, *The Fijitive* provides a window into the emotional state of the 18th General Hospital and the feelings and attitudes of its members. Although the paper is unfailingly upbeat, negative emotions occasionally emerge through the façade. One such feeling is restlessness. After being essentially trapped on a small island for roughly two years, and being idle for much of that time, many people in the 18th were itching to leave Fiji. For instance, in his article about the horrors of seaborne transportation in the military, Sgt. Kehoe wrote that if he were allowed to leave the next day on that same ship, "you would find me scrambling up the side before they could place the gangplank" (ibid.). In addition, the reader quickly gets the sense that the 18th's members were generally unhappy with their role in the war and wished that their considerable skills were not so underutilized. This sentiment is stated most clearly in a May 26 editorial in which a Colonel George Finney wrote that many members of the 18th General Hospital felt that they were not doing their part in the war effort (Finney 1).

Though only intended to be read by those in the unit, *The Fijitive* has much to offer readers today. In addition to providing ample comic relief, the newspaper illuminates aspects of the 18th's experience that are ignored in Tilghman's *L.O.D.—Yes*, and to a lesser extent in letters home. Hence, while not offering a comprehensive narrative, *The Fijitive* is revealing in its own right and is essential for a more complete understanding of the wartime service of the 18th General Hospital.

Letters from the 18th

Letters written by members of the 18th General Hospital, most of which were published in *The Johns Hopkins Nurses Alumnae Magazine*, are also invaluable sources of information. The 1943 and 1944 issues of this quarterly publication featured letters written by several of the unit's nurses. Almost all of these letters, and by far the most compelling of them, were authored by Elizabeth McLaughlin. A 1937 graduate of the Johns Hopkins School of Nursing, McLaughlin signed up to serve the 18th General Hospital in 1940. She also volunteered to be a "special Alumnae Magazine correspondent" of the *Nurses Alumnae Magazine*, which meant she was tasked with writing letters to the magazine for publication, providing its readers with news of the overseas unit.[8] She performed this task admirably, keeping the Johns Hopkins community abreast of the 18th's exploits. More than that, however, her charming series of letters sheds further light on the wartime experience of the 18th General Hospital, primarily due to her unique perspective.

Although the subject matter of her letters and *The Fijitive* overlap considerably, McLaughlin addresses several aspects of the unit's experience on which *The Fijitive*'s contributors neglected to report. Namely, she discusses the appearance and layout of the hospital facility and living quarters, the rapid and improvised construction of said buildings, the sweltering and at times tempestuous weather of Fiji, and devotes a considerable part of her correspondence to describing the native Fijians with whom members of the unit frequently interacted.[9]

She characterizes Fijians as primitive yet joyful people "who have bodies like Greek statues and who walk like gods."[10] She finds their lack of self-consciousness endearing, though she admits that their laid-back ways could sometimes cause frustration, such as when the unit's Fijian domestic help, after being told that the inspectors were en route, decided to take a leisurely stroll instead of cleaning the living quarters.[11] In addition, McLaughlin reports on some of the native customs that initially bewildered the Americans. One example is the tradition of burying a placenta under a tree immediately after childbirth in order to keep track of the child's age.[12] She also describes the drinking of *kava*, a beverage derived from the root of the Kava plant that is customarily imbibed in a ceremony welcoming visitors. When a member of the 18th would come upon an indigenous village he or she would have to participate in a ceremony where "one at a time, the participants, seated in a circle, drink the *kava* from half coconut shells to the rhythmic clapping of hands." Immediately after drinking, "one is expected to spin the cup on the ground and utter a grunt of deep satisfaction."[13] Although the drink was purported by the Fijians to have a sedative effect, McLaughlin wrote that she was unable to detect anything of the sort.[14] It is her discussion of topics such as these that makes her letters so compelling and allows them to stand out from the other sources.

The way in which McLaughlin writes her letters is further illuminating. Her writing style is quite descriptive, and the depictions of daily life for the 18th General Hospital are eminently detailed and vivid. To illustrate, in the July 1943 issue of the *Nurses Alumnae Magazine* she takes the reader on a tour of the unit's encampment, beginning with the medical wards:

> Walking down toward "Tent City" we see in addition to some remaining tents, long frame wards, each holding sixty patients. The high pitched whistle you hear being blown by a patient walking from ward to ward is the mess call for ambulatory patients. In a moment, shining mess kits in hand, the boys will run, not walk, to the long tent furnished with well scrubbed boards and benches. Keggy Lewis's tented "field kitchen" does a boom-time business with gasoline stove and GI cans.[15]

She next escorts the reader past the enlisted men's recreation hut, the physiotherapy tent, the officers' area, and finishes at the nurses' quarters. McLaughlin's writing style allows the reader to easily and vividly visualize the places she is describing. In this regard she is unmatched; no other author of a primary source concerning the 18th did this as well as she.

The fact that McLaughlin is a woman likely contributes significantly to the narrative of the 18th General Hospital's experience overseas. This is because she discusses what are traditionally considered "feminine" subjects that *The Fijitive* and *L.O.D.—Yes* completely ignore. For instance, she describes the standard-issue army nurse's uniform in some detail ("blue wool skirts and not-so-white blouses," oversized raincoats and rubber boots for the rain) and wonders if the fashion preferences of the nurses would change as a result of wearing the same uniform day in and day out.[16] She additionally illustrates for those reading at home the clothing and hairstyles worn by the Fijians as well. In her usual vivid style she describes the latest native hairstyles:

> With the Fijian, beauty starts at the top. In 1944 the style of Fijian men is to have the hair cut three inches long all over the head except for the back which is trimmed like an English wig. The three inches stand straight up, —the grizzlier the aspect the better. The women model their hairstyles after the men, but they retain more of the natural kinkiness. They are enthusiasts for variation in the color scheme. Red hair comes from the juice of the mangrove bark. Limed hair originated from the necessity of overcoming bug infestation when lime mixed with water was used. Besides eradicating the bugs, the new light color delighted the hosts.[17]

These are topics other sources do not even touch upon, and yet McLaughlin discusses them in significant depth. Consequently, McLaughlin's feminine perspective may have had a role in her correspondence's ability to fill in the holes of the 18th's wartime experience left by the other sources.

In her series of letters, McLaughlin attempted to grant those not part of the unit a window into the lives of the unit's members. While they offer neither the wealth of detailed information of *L.O.D.—Yes* nor the comic relief of *The Fijitive,* her letters are uniquely informative. By revealing aspects of her daily life that other sources ignore, Elizabeth McLaughlin's letters to *The Johns Hopkins Nurses Alumnae Magazine* help provide a fuller picture of the experience of the 18th General Hospital during World War II.

The Legacy of the 18th

Clearly evident from these sources is the fact that the wartime experience of the 18th General Hospital did not go as its members had hoped. They wished to do something similar to the lifesaving medicine performed by their forebears in World War I, and wanted all of the glory, intensity, and satisfaction that go along with such work (Turner 488). But as the reader well knows at this point, this was not to be. For much of the war, the 18th General Hospital saw few patients, even fewer wounded soldiers, and spent much of its time professionally idle. But the 18th's service was certainly not a wasted enterprise. Even though the unit was largely unable to do what it had set out to do, its circumstances, actions, and accomplishments were remarkable nonetheless.

The profound disappointment felt by many in the 18th General Hospital certainly had much to do with unfulfilled expectations. What likely formed the basis of these preconceptions was the experience of a Johns Hopkins-affiliated hospital unit in the First World War. This unit, Base Hospital No. 18, was the first medical unit from a civilian university to embark overseas. In 1917 the U.S. Army dispatched the unit as part the American Expeditionary Force to northeastern France (Turner 32). Just a few tens of miles behind the western front, Base Hospital No. 18 provided lifesaving surgical care to wounded American soldiers around the clock. According to Johns Hopkins historian Thomas Turner, members of that unit found their work "exhausting, exhilarating, and satisfying" (33). When the unit returned home, its members were lauded as heroes and their valiant service soon became legendary in the Johns Hopkins community (34).

Due to this precedent, members of the 18th General Hospital, which was named in homage of their predecessors, could be forgiven for expecting something similar. Excitement began to build soon after the announcement came in 1940 that Hopkins would likely again send some of its own overseas to serve in the military (Turner 483). The fact that one of the two units would bear the same designation of the legendary World War I outfit generated further enthusiasm and was a source of great pride within the Hopkins community. It also, however, meant that expectations would be particularly high for the 18th, and its successes would be measured against those of its predecessor (Turner 484). Positions in the two units were quickly filled by eager volunteers who, excited to serve their country, hoped for an early activation (Jones 36). After the Pearl Harbor attacks they received their wish. On a rainy night in Baltimore, both the 18th and 118th General Hospitals departed to great fanfare, with everyone present hoping for something of a sequel to the heroics of twenty-five years prior (Turner 484).

Almost immediately, however, the 18th learned that their journey would differ significantly in at least one respect. Instead of heading for Europe, where the unit wished to serve, it headed west, towards the Pacific theater. This was a definite disappointment for the 18th because it would not be following in the footsteps of the previous Hopkins unit, and would be embarking for a part of the world, according to Turner, "with which most of [its] members were unfamiliar and in which their interest was meager" (Turner 485).

Once the 18th arrived in Fiji, all indications were that it would be quite busy. The Army high command in the Pacific believed that Fiji would be of great strategic importance and that a Japanese invasion of the archipelago was a definite possibility (Tilghman 1). Also, the American invasion of Guadalcanal and Tulagi was scheduled to begin just four days after the 18th's arrival. After landing in Fiji, however, the 18th was not able to accept patients for several weeks, due to the fact that a hospital facility had to be built from the ground up. When the hospital was finally operational, those in the 18th did get the chance to treat battle casualties and were quite busy. Within several months, however, casualties ceased flowing into Fiji and the 18th's patient census fell drastically. Fiji was also never attacked due to the decisive American victories at Midway and the Coral Sea, which put the Japanese navy irrevocably on the defensive. By mid-1943, the war had simply passed the 18th General Hospital by. Many of the soldiers treated by the hospital at this point had already undergone the necessary surgery at a hospital closer to the front, and were sent to Fiji merely to recover from their wounds (Tilghman 12-24).

When the 18th was ordered to pack up and leave Fiji for deployment elsewhere, there was hope within the unit that they would now become more professionally active and involved in the war effort. Again, however, their destination was a disappointment. Instead of traveling northwest towards the Philippines and the Japanese home islands, where the major American offensives were focused, the 18th General Hospital was sent in a more westerly direction to India. Once the 18th arrived at their station in Ledo, Assam, in the India-Burma theater, morale sunk to new depths. After coming from an idyllic island paradise with a full-fledged hospital installation, the unsavory conditions and thoroughly dilapidated buildings in India were a difficult pill to swallow (Tilghman 28-34). Lieutenant Jean Hays referred to their new situation as "a mess after Fiji" and Major C.C. Troland, a medical officer in the 18th, described their new duty station as "really a bit of a hell hole" (Mura 276; Hill). Furthermore, there were already hospital units operating in the immediate vicinity that were more than able to handle the current patient load. Although the unit was somewhat busy in Ledo, it was only because they had to spend much of their time repairing their run-down facility. The members of the 18th General Hospital were professionally idle for almost the entirety of their stay on the subcontinent and were saved from further frustration and boredom by a sympathetic General Frank Merrill, who, appalled at their plight, arranged for the rotation home of all the remaining members from Johns Hopkins University (Tilghman 34-38).

The oppressively low morale that resulted from this clash of expectations with reality took its toll on the members of the unit. According to "The Tattler" in the August 3 issue of *The Fijitive*, a common complaint of those in the 18th was: "Another six months and I'll blow my top." Jean Hays wrote that in Ledo quite a few people in the unit seriously considered faking or exaggerating an illness in order to be sent home, and that some may have even done so (Mura 282, 294). Some in the 18th wrote songs and poems expressing their unhappiness and their strong desire to escape from their miserable situation, which was usually achieved via rotation to a stateside unit. One poem, written by Sergeant Al Weber, an enlisted man in the 18th, expressed these sentiments in rhyme:

> Here I am waitin'
> Speculatin' and debatin'
> Just when I'll be ratin'
> Rotatin'!
> For Rotatin' is belatin'
> And I'm being frank in statin'
> That I am really hatin'
> This waitin'!
> Rotatin'! Belatin'! – Hatin'!
> This waitin'!
> Answer? See Satan!!! (Weber)

By no means was their service all for naught, however. Although the 18th did not achieve what they had set out to do, their accomplishments were certainly notable. In addition for caring for American servicemen, the 18th served also as a hospital for both Fijian soldiers and civilians. The unit was designed to exclusively care for American servicemen, but due to the dramatic decrease in the patient load during 1944, it was able to provide valuable medical care for the islanders (Tilghman 24). In some cases, doctors and nurses of the 18th would accompany public health workers, who were usually British, to remote villages in order to treat and inoculate those who were ordinarily too far removed from population centers to receive adequate medical care. The service provided to the Fijians was considerable. Indeed, Sir Philip Mitchell, the Governor of Fiji, sent a letter to the commanding officer of the 18th's task force expressing his deep gratitude for the services provided by the unit to the population of Fiji (Tilghman 25).

Doctors of the 18th General Hospital also made critical contributions to the medical knowledge of the time. First, they observed that all circumstances being equal, wounds healed just as well in tropical areas as they did in more temperate regions, an observation that went against the conventional medical opinion of the 1940s. Second, Captain Roger Lewis, one of the 18th's doctors, discovered a method of detecting the amount of atabrine in a patient's body. Due to the fact that quinine was non-existent in the Pacific theater, atabrine was the drug of choice for combating malaria, which was very common in the Southwest Pacific. A significant drawback of atabrine, however, was that it was dangerously toxic in high doses. Being able to determine the amount of the drug already present in a patient's bloodstream helped caregivers reduce overdoses to a minimum. As a result, Lewis's discovery was vital to the military's battle against malaria in the Pacific Theatre. Thus, although such contributions are overlooked amongst the overall backdrop of disappointment, they were certainly valuable to the war effort (ibid., 22-25; Turner 486-487).

The fact that the 18th General Hospital was in a place like Fiji was extraordinary in and of itself. As mentioned earlier, the unit initially had little interest in an isolated and little-heard-of group of islands in the middle of the Pacific Ocean. Few, if any, members of the unit had been to a location like Fiji previous to their war service, and were awed by the its picturesque beauty as a result. Authors in the 18th such as Tilghman and McLaughlin wrote at length about the tropical paradise that was their home, in turn allowing their readers to appreciate Fiji's splendor.

Another noteworthy feature of the 18th General Hospital's three-year tenure overseas was the frequent and amiable interactions with people very different from the unit's personnel. Initially, the American hospital unit did not know what to expect of the native people of Fiji and wondered how westernized they had become as a result of British dominion over the archipelago. To illustrate, in one of her letters Elizabeth McLaughlin writes that upon arriving, "we expected to cut our way through the bush with care to avoid the headquarters of the cannibal industry."[18] This turned out not be the case. Although a somewhat primitive people by western standards, the natives were extraordinarily friendly towards the Americans from the start. Soon enough, the Fijians and the Americans developed a congenial relationship, associating so closely that some of the enlisted men often brought Fijian women to dances hosted by the 18th (the nurses, as commissioned officers, were off-limits to the enlisted men).[19]

As a result of the genuinely friendly relationship with the Fijians, the unit's portrayals of them were overwhelmingly positive. First, by all accounts the Fijians were considered quite good-looking by the members of the 18th. For instance, a contributor to *The Fijitive* vividly remembered the first dance at which he was "introduced to the beautiful females of Fiji."[20] Second, those in the 18th also appeared to have tremendous respect for the culture and way of life of the Fijian peoples. In the case of Elizabeth McLaughlin, her admiration for the indigenous culture caused her to doubt the supposed merits of her own. In her October 1943 letter, she writes:

> There was probably never a lovelier world than that of the islands uncontaminated by the white man, who came uninvited to give them the dubious gifts of civilization: firearms, disease, and the mores of religion. After a year of observing the remaining vestiges of an old, idyllic civilization, we wonder about what we call "culture."[21]

This degree of admiration for the Fijians on the part of the Americans is somewhat surprising considering that America was in many ways a racist society during this time, particularly south of the Mason-Dixon line, from which many in the unit hailed. Furthermore, in recent years the war in the Pacific has been classified as a race war, in which each side was fueled by racist hatred towards the other (Dower). In light of this as well it is both a surprise and a relief that such sentiments are not in evidence in any of the sources examined in this paper.

Another distinguishing aspect of the 18th's experience was its members' extraordinary penchant for finding and creating ways to entertain themselves. In addition to publishing a weekly newspaper, members of the unit organized both men's and women's teams in several different sports, and later formed leagues in which clubs from the 18th would compete with those of like their military units stationed on Fiji.[22] They staged and performed in dances, concerts, and plays, and held several much larger events like the two County Fairs and the Minstrel Show.[23] Many members of the 18th also would go on lengthy sightseeing excursions (sometimes a week or more) to beaches, other islands in the Fiji archipelago, or even to places as far away as Samoa.[24] In addition to being essential for the maintenance of any semblance of morale, these activities were a noteworthy feature of the experience of the 18th General Hospital.

Although disappointment due to unfulfilled expectations is readily apparent in the writings of those in the 18th General Hospital, it does not paint a complete picture of the unit's overseas service. By looking past the backdrop of negativity the reader can recognize that the 18th's experience was a remarkable one. The unit made significant contributions to the war effort and health of the local population, resided in a singularly beautiful locale, was startlingly open-minded, and partook in an uncommon variety of leisure activities. Perhaps some of the disappointment felt by those in the 18th is unwarranted after all.

Conclusion

The plight of the 18th General Hospital is probably not what comes to mind when one thinks of a military medical unit. Its men and women do not fit the romantic image of the courageous medic braving enemy fire to perform first aid on his comrade, or of the battlefield surgeon saving gravely wounded soldiers from the brink of death in the midst of a warzone. For most of the war, those in the 18th simply sat idle on a pristine island paradise in the middle of the Pacific and devoted much of their time to pursuits other than saving lives. The fact that the experience of the unit went against the grain is what makes it so noteworthy and fascinating to outsiders.

This paper represents an attempt to capture a moment in time experienced by a particular group of people. Within it three distinct primary source bases, including two that have likely never been previously employed in scholarly writing, are used to construct both a richer and more cohesive narrative of the experience of the 18th General Hospital. In addition, the paper serves as a challenge to how this moment in time was perceived by those in the unit, and by extension the authors of secondary literature on the subject. Although

Thomas Turner, in his definitive history of the Johns Hopkins Medical Institutions, labels the 18th's overseas odyssey as an "unhappy saga" (488), this paper demonstrates that such an epithet does not do the unit justice. Whether the experience of the 18th General Hospital was typical of hospital units in World War II and whether parallels can be drawn to the experience of the 18th's sister unit, the 118th General Hospital, are questions that invite further research.

Works Cited

Condon-Rall, Mary, and Albert E. Cowdrey. *The Medical Department: Medical Service in the War Against Japan.* Washington: U.S. Government Publishing Office, 1998.

Doster, Daphne. *Johns Hopkins Nursing Historical Collection*, Box 505718. *The Alan Mason Chesney Medical Archives*, Baltimore, Maryland.

Dower, John. *War Without Mercy: Race and Power in the Pacific War.* NY: Pantheon Books, 1986.

Finney, George. "A Message From Our Commanding Officer." *The Fijitive* (26 May 1944): 1.

Graham, Richard. "Greetings." *The Fijitive*, 29 March, 1944: 1.

Hill, Carroll. Box 505758. *The Alan Mason Chesney Medical Archives*, Baltimore, Maryland.

Jones, H. Alvan. "The 18th General Hospital." *The Johns Hopkins Nurses Alumnae Magazine* 43.2 (1944): 36.

Kehoe, M. "A Letter to the Editors." *The Fijitive*, 26 May, 1944: 4.

McLaughlin, Elizabeth. "Behind the Scenes with General Hospital No. 18." *The Johns Hopkins Nurses Alumni Magazine* 42.1 (1943).

Mura, Tiffany. *The Diary of Jean Hays: A WWII Army Nurse in Fiji.* Bridgewater, NJ: Replica Books, 2006.

Ross, R. S. "R. Carmichael Tilghman 1904-1999." *Transactions of the American Clinical and Climatological Association* 111 (2000): lv-lvii. http://www.ncbi.nlm.nih.gov/pmc/articles/PMC2194362/. Accessed March 31st, 2010.

"The Tattler," *The Fijitive*, 3 August, 1944: 3.

Tilghman, R. Carmichael. *L.O.D.—Yes: An Odyssey of the Army's 18th General Hospital.* Baltimore: The Johns Hopkins University Press, 1947.

Turner, Thomas. *Heritage of Excellence: The Johns Hopkins Medical Institutions, 1914-1947.* Baltimore: The Johns Hopkins University Press, 1974.

Weber, Al. "Rotatin'!," *The Fijitive*, 17 August, 1944: 3.

Endnotes

1 Elizabeth McLaughlin, "Behind the Scenes with General Hospital No. 18."

The Johns Hopkins Nurses Alumni Magazine 42, no. 1 (1943): 16. Due to the number of citations from McLaughlin's columns, her work will be cited in endnote form.
2 Ibid., 13.
3 Ibid., 14.
4 Ibid., 16.
5 Elizabeth McLaughlin, "Hopkins News from the Armed Forces." *The Johns Hopkins Nurses Alumnae Magazine* 42, no. 4 (1943): 170.
6 McLaughlin, *The Johns Hopkins Nurses Alumnae Magazine* 42, no. 1 (1943): 15.
7 Elizabeth McLaughlin, "Behind the Scenes with General Hospital No. 18." *The Johns Hopkins Nurses Alumni Magazine* 43, no. 3 (1944): 84, 85
8 "Captain Stafford from General Hospital #18 Visits Baltimore." *The Johns Hopkins Nurses Alumnae Magazine* 42, no. 2 (1943): 12.
9 McLaughlin, *The Johns Hopkins Nurses Alumnae Magazine* 42, no. 1 (1943): 16; McLaughlin, "From General Hospitals 18 and 118." *The Johns Hopkins Nurses Alumnae Magazine* 42, no. 3 (1943): 96, 97.
10 Elizabeth McLaughlin, "Hopkins News from the Armed Forces." *The Johns Hopkins Nurses Alumnae Magazine* 43, no. 2 (1944): 44.
11 McLaughlin, *The Johns Hopkins Nurses Alumnae Magazine* 42, no. 3 (1943): 95.
12 McLaughlin, *The Johns Hopkins Nurses Alumnae Magazine* 42, no. 4 (1943): 169.
13 McLaughlin, *The Johns Hopkins Nurses Alumnae Magazine* 43, no. 2 (1944): 43.
14 Ibid.
15 McLaughlin, *The Johns Hopkins Nurses Alumnae Magazine* 42, no. 3 (1943): 96, 97.
16 McLaughlin, *The Johns Hopkins Nurses Alumnae Magazine* 42, no. 1 (1943): 15.
17 McLaughlin, *The Johns Hopkins Nurses Alumnae Magazine* 43, no. 3 (1944): 84, 85.
18 McLaughlin, *The Johns Hopkins Nurses Alumnae Magazine* 43, no. 2 (1944): 43.
19 Ibid., 45.
20 "The Tattler," *The Fijitive*, 26 May, 1944, 6.
21 McLaughlin, *The Johns Hopkins Nurses Alumnae Magazine* 42, no. 4 (1943): 168.
22 McLaughlin, *The Johns Hopkins Nurses Alumnae Magazine* 43, no. 3 (1944): 84, 85
23 "July 4th County Fair A Wow," *The Fijitive*, 6 July, 1944, 1.
24 McLaughlin, *The Johns Hopkins Nurses Alumnae Magazine* 43, no. 3 (1944): 83.

Shaving with the Grain: Portraying an Effective Iago

Tony Levero
Loyola University Maryland

Note from Professor Bryan Crockett, Loyola University Maryland: Tony Levero's essay is an example of a "staging paper," an assignment I sometimes give in drama classes. In the paper's first section the student researches and comments on the effectiveness of previous staged or filmed productions of a play, then decides on an interpretation of a very small portion of the text: ten to fifteen lines of dialogue. The student defends this interpretation, explaining why it would work more effectively on stage than would others. In the second section the student divides the passage into "beats": small units of speech in which the character exhibits particular motives for choosing exactly these words, delivering them with the intonations and body language the student decides upon. After each beat the student explains in practice how the theory described in the paper's first section is effectively embodied on the stage.

The primary staging concern for any director producing a version of *Othello* should be the choices his actor takes in portraying Iago. For the passage I have chosen—Act 3, Scene 3, lines 110-120—this performance is particularly crucial to the balance of the production. Iago embodies the vice character of medieval morality plays. A far cry from such one-dimensional creations as Titivillus, Iago displays actual depth, charm, and humor in dialogue. He stands as a representation of the dexterity Shakespeare commands in bringing a villain to the stage that both amuses and horrifies the audience.

Tony Levero is in his junior year as an English and Political Science major at Loyola University Maryland, where he contributes to several campus publications including: *Warnings*, *The Garland*, and *The Greyhound*.

The passage chosen stands in the center of the drama. It represents a miniature of the overall manipulation that Iago works throughout the play on his superior Othello. For the actor, an "honest" portrayal of the character at this juncture is pivotal for delivering an effective performance.

The key to producing an effective Iago is a balance of both subtlety and honesty of demeanor. A mature audience will be able to discern a villain without capering, sniveling, or the ever-obvious pyrotechnics that accompanied more rudimentary vice characters of earlier theater. The dialogue Shakespeare has written for him never deviates from what other characters could believe without seeming naïve or stupid to the audience. Neither should the actions chosen by an actor stray from this realism.

Daniel Seltzer characterizes this realism as an "emphasis on roughness, frankness, and an honest lack of polish, all professed by Iago to be his true traits" (204). Seltzer also points out that given "the direction his speech will take, we must remember that his mask, his *persona,* is completed by the fact that he is a soldier" (204). This practical portrayal speaks to a more realistic character than the morality plays would have used. This keeps present in the viewers' minds the idea that Iago does indeed have motivations behind his evil: "For Iago's pathetic character, the tragedy lies in the fact that he allows his emotions to usurp his reason" (McCloskey 27). This insight is key. In dialogue, it is important for the actor to remember that Iago may possess control over his emotions when speaking but is still subject to their influence in his actions (they are his "vice," if you will). Relegating him to the unrealistic does Shakespeare an injustice: "It is not sufficient to simply drape Iago in allegorical trappings and proclaim him Mister Evil or a Machiavel or a Vice. Such a limited view of Iago is an injustice to the complexity of his character since Shakespeare's studies in personality are acclaimed by psychologists" (West 27). While West makes a valid point that Iago improves upon these vice characters, it is a fairly uncontested point, since it would take a neophyte of an actor to mistake Iago for such a shallow character. Also, a simple examination of the text by any reader should prove Iago a complex character, without the assistance of psychologists.

While few actors would make the error of portraying such a shallow, Machiavellian Iago, the temptation to overact his dialogue is a common one. In some productions, a departure from realism in favor of over-the-top "ham" acting has drawn poor reaction from audiences and critics. This type of actor may ad lib or play to the crowd too heavily, lacking any subtlety or attention to the little details. In this way, they do not really improve upon the villains of earlier dramas. Charles B. Lower describes an Alliance production of *Othello* in which a movie actor, Richard Dreyfuss, portrayed such an Iago. Lower describes the audience reaction: "Blind to his demonic potential, most reviewers saw only the comedic, against which they railed. Playing his 'lengthier soliloquies straight to the crowd, Dreyfuss appears to be having a ball, but this breaking out of character hampers the flow and concentration of the play'"(Lower 219). While Lower defends this decision made by Dreyfuss as crucial to contrasting the later heaviness of the tragedy, the unpopularity with audiences is understandable. A caricature is an ineffective way to portray such a multidimensional villain.

Othello, the main object of Iago's manipulation, must possess several traits in order to make Iago's portrayal successful. "Thus the main impression we get of Othello is the one Samuel Johnson describes as, 'magnanimous, artless and credulous, boundless in his confidence, ardent in his affection'" (Schwartz 298). While Othello is quite intelligent and capable, his ego will lend him the credulity he needs in order to believably fall victim to Iago's arts. The fact that Iago cedes authority to him (in word at least) should be more than enough to buy the trust of Othello.

In staging the scene, a variety of approaches have been taken. In film, greater liberties are allowed. Orson Welles portrays the dialogue taking place while Othello and Iago simply walk along a parapet. A stage production would not have access to this type of set, and I believe that Welles failed to properly utilize the possibilities lent to him by the film medium. In the Laurence Fishburne version of *Othello*, the dialogue is staggered over a variety of activities that could not possibly take place within the amount of time that elapses in the dialogue (Barron and Roeg). These actions would be fairly mundane for soldiers like Iago and Othello and, therefore, add some verisimilitude to the lines being delivered. However, the lapse of time would not work realistically on stage and therefore would have to be reduced to only one activity in order to work. I take this element from Fishburne's version and eliminate the impractical.

Act 3 Scene 3 lines 110-120

My Staging: The stage should be thrust, with house lights on. This was the manner in which Shakespeare's company would have performed the play. It gives the audience several angles from which to view the action. No tricks with stage lighting should be necessary in order to effectively portray the action in this scene. Bathing the audience in the same light as the actors gives them an additional involvement in the action of the play, reducing the sense of the "fourth wall."

Once Desdemona and Emilia exit, Iago should undertake some activity that denotes Othello's authority over him. A big part of Iago's ability to manipulate his military leader comes from his ability to flatter. Othello will feel more secure and trustful if Iago is doing a particularly subservient duty for him. This action should also serve to limit Othello's freedom of motion. By making Othello stationary, the *true* balance of power should shift to Iago, who can take advantage of his mobility.

A variety of acts could be useful here. Iago could shine Othello's shoes, dress him, or polish his armor. However, for this scene I would stage Iago shaving Othello.[1] The power dynamic of one man shaving another has been utilized to great effect as a central plot device in both Hernando Téllez's short story "Just Lather, That's All" and Steven Sondheim's musical *Sweeney Todd*. This works particularly well for this play, since Othello cannot move his head. Iago will insinuate things that provoke Othello's impatience and jealousy, but Othello will be unable to move. Iago would be aware of Othello's propensity for rage and be particularly aware of Othello's potential to dominate him physically. However, the slightest motion may cause Iago's razor to slip, making Othello powerless in this respect. Othello ought to be aware of the danger, though it should be noted that he trusts and respects Iago here.

Furthermore, the act of shaving would play to the director's advantage. Since most of Iago's blocking would take place behind Othello, Iago would be able to make all sorts of gestures and expressions while Othello would remain oblivious, staring forward. His inability to read Iago's expressions adds further fuel to his frustration, as he is forced to speculate on the meaning of the villain's words.

---

1   The notion of Othello being shaven comes from a production of the play starring an actor, Ethan Stone, as Otello. This scene was posted on YouTube.

Othello sits in a chair with a small table of toiletries behind and stage right of him. Iago stands behind and works from these items: a basin of water, towels, shaving cream, and a straight razor.

Othello: Why of thy thought Iago?

Iago has asked whether Cassio was aware of Othello and Desdemona's relationship. Othello answers affirmatively and questions the reason behind Iago's curiosity. Iago easily shrugs off Othello's counter-question and attributes his own question to idle curiosity.

Still, Othello is curious. He should not be angry or even suspicious yet, just a conversational level of interest. The line should be delivered briefly and at a relatively high pitch (relative to the actor at least, most adaptations choose an actor with a deeper voice than the man who plays Iago). His pitch should rise when he speaks Iago's name, denoting the question.

Iago: I did not think he had been acquainted with her

Iago should deliver this line briefly. However, he should pause and put a brief inflection on the word "acquainted." Any mature audience member should be able to pick up on the innuendo associated with "acquaint." The word had, at the time, (and still does) the connotation of experimental knowledge: "mutually known; having personal or experimental knowledge of" (*Oxford English Dictionary*, adj. definition number 1.a). For a jealous husband, it would be a logical step to assume that this experimental knowledge may be sexual in nature. Iago subtly but purposefully introduces the notion of infidelity. He will slowly but surely make the accusation more obvious. Also, the actor should note that this is the first time Iago uses the word "think." He should be aware that this word will be a sticking point for Othello later in the scene, as he becomes impatient and demands knowledge of Iago's thoughts.

Iago should busy himself covering Othello in shaving cream. He should do so briskly, crossing from one shoulder to another, pausing only to deliver the word "acquainted," with a nod. Possibly, Iago just realizes the sexual implication of the word himself while saying it, and is pleased by this. It is important that he seem thoroughly occupied in his task, though, trying not to arouse too much suspicion in Othello just yet.

Othello: O yes, and went between us very oft.

This should be the last line that Othello delivers so naïvely. The crucial word of this line is "between." It may connote two meanings. Othello is referring to the fact that Cassio delivered messages *between* him and Desdemona. However, in an alternate meaning, this sentence could denote that Cassio *came* between them. Rather than simply traveling between them, Cassio may have driven a wedge between them sexually, or simply emotionally. By being "between" them, he could be an obstacle between the couple in their marriage. Othello has stated indirectly that very thing which Iago is attempting to bait him into believing.

Here, Iago should immediately pause, midway into his first stroke across Othello's left cheek. A glimmer should enter his face. Othello has given him an opening to exploit. For a villain of his caliber, the actor should portray the face of a child unwrapping the plumpest Christmas present of his life.

Iago: Indeed?

Iago delivers this line with a feigned incredulity that should be slightly notable for the audience in its falseness. He attempts to bait Othello into believing that he retains some knowledge that he does not. By doing so, Othello will believe that Iago knows something of Cassio's comings and goings between the couple.

Iago should hurriedly resume his shaving, pretending to not want suspicion aroused. He should place his hand directly on top of Othello's head, to steady it and limit motion.

Othello: Indeed? Ay, indeed. Discern'st thou aught in that?

Finally, Othello catches on to Iago's hints. He should first deliver "indeed" simply as an echo of Iago. The conversation is now moving quicker, at a pace difficult for Othello to keep. By echoing Iago he is perhaps buying time until he can process the way in which Iago used the word "indeed." Next, he discerns the source of Iago's feigned disbelief and redelivers "Ay, indeed" thoughtfully, almost as if to reassure himself. He should take a beat before "discern'st."

Here he should assume the deep tone of a leader who can demand information from a subordinate.

He attempts to turn to see Iago on this line, but Iago holds his head still once again, and begins shaving his right cheek, lower to the jawline and neck.

Is he not honest?

Failing to turn and see Iago, Othello resumes attempting to interrogate him with words rather than looks. As a military leader he would have interrogated many men and it should come naturally to him. His voice retains the strong tone of a commander. He delivers the word "honest" in its strictly ethical sense. He may not have realized the full meaning of Iago's behavior yet and simply believes that Iago is calling Cassio's general morals into question. Perhaps Othello has not made the full connection between these general moral shortcomings that Iago implies and Cassio's comings and goings between himself and Desdemona.

He has given up seeing Iago and remains stoically set forward. With each stroke, Iago works closer to his throat. He is completely enveloped in his work, forgetting the audience for the moment, and leaning in so close as to deliver his next line directly in Othello's ear.

Iago: Honest, my lord?

Iago should deliver the word "honest" in a soft, barely audible undertone, one that denotes the double entendre. While Othello had used the word in its traditional context, Iago will now play off of the fact that it can also mean "chaste, 'virtuous'" (*OED*: adj. definition number 3.b). He has moved from the realm of generalities of Cassio's character and has specifically called his sexual morality into question. He should deliver the words "my lord" in a raised voice, one that flatters Othello's desire to be respected.

He cedes respect to Othello's authority via words, all the while maintaining his own, situational authority as the wielder of the razor. He is now so close to Othello's ear as to make his whisper seem suggestive. The rage of jealousy Othello will feel from this line should be seductive to Iago.

Othello: Honest—Ay, honest.

Othello delivers the first "honest" as a legitimate question, a hopeful chance for Iago to clarify the manner in which he seemed to place insinuation on the word. He should leave an awkwardly long beat in which Iago continues shaving but the villain says nothing to ameliorate his implication.

Finally, after painful silence, Othello repeats with grave stress the word "honest." This time, he delivers the word with absolute clarity, accepting Iago's accusation reluctantly. Here, Iago slows his work and looks up to see the audience, finally removing his mouth from such close proximity to his lord's ear. He should wear a face of power and satisfaction.

Iago: My lord, for aught I know

Again, he appeals to Othello's pride through his title. He delivers the line tersely. The most significant aspect of this line is that he offers reassurance without *real* reassurance. The audience and Othello should note that he does not promise Cassio's honesty. He simply says that Cassio is honest to the extent of his own knowledge. It is notable that Iago tells the truth here as he does with consistency throughout the play, something that sets him apart from many villains of the time (including many of Shakespeare's). He has no ocular proof to the contrary, but he allows the possibility that his own knowledge is limited. Othello is an impatient man and would have hoped that Iago owned some exclusive knowledge that Othello could pry from him immediately. By denying any insight Iago teases Othello further, as he must now wait and gather facts elsewhere.

Iago should pause his work completely, all the while leaving the blade fixed on Othello's neck. Othello's frustration is now obvious to the audience as his jealousy builds.

Othello: What dost thou think?

Othello finally loses his composure on this line. He shouts it though he remains still. He places special inflection on the word "thou." He demands full disclosure of Iago's *personal* feelings on Cassio, something that Iago appears hesitant to grant.

Iago: Think, my lord?

Iago's face should reveal satisfaction. The psychological balance of power is completely in his hands now. He has no more use for the razor and tosses it into the basin. He proceeds to grab a hot towel and busily begin wiping the cream from Othello's face, even if stubble remains. Noticeable to the audience, this should be somewhat comical. Perhaps the poor job of shaving is characteristic of Iago, who may not be of a class used to such menial labor. He should return to his feigned ignorance, focused intently on his task of Othello's hygiene.

Iago delivers this last line in an understated and put-on, oblivious manner. He has planted the seed of jealousy and no longer needs to drop hints. Othello, who may have believed that he was close to discerning Iago's thoughts earlier, should now stand up in frustration.

Conclusion

By stripping the stage and props to bare necessities, the audience is treated to a theater experience free of distraction from the actors' qualities. The razor adds a bump to the dramatic tension that did not exist to this extent in the film versions of the play that were mentioned above. It lubricates the dialogue by adding a previously unexplored power dynamic. Through a proper staging that allows Iago room to exploit his character to the fullest, the dramatic experience of the entire work of *Othello* is enhanced. Stroke for stroke, he stands among the greatest villains in literature.

Works Cited

Barron, David and Roeg, Luc. *Othello*. Columbia Pictures, 1995.

Lower, Charles B. "An Alliance *Othello*." *Shakespeare Quarterly* 31.2 (1980): 218-220.

McCloskey, John C. "An Alliance Othello." *College English* 3.1 (1941): 25-30.

Seltzer, Daniel. "Elizabethan Acting in *Othello*." *Shakespeare Quarterly* 10.2 (1959): 201-210.

Schwartz, Elias. "Stylistic 'Impurity' and the Meaning of *Othello*." *Studies in English Literature, 1500-1900* 10.2 (1970): 297-313.

Welles, Orson. *Othello*. Mercury Productions Inc., 1952.
West, Fred. "Iago the Psychopath." *South Atlantic Bulletin* 43.2 (1978): 27-35.

Reviewing the Various Stages of Shakespeare's *Macbeth*

Jennifer L. Bryant
Frostburg State University

Directors usually have a keen idea of how they wish to pursue a theater production in a way which may or may not be different from both proceeding and succeeding conceptions. At the same time, while some similarities may exist, the themes of all productions hold some sort of key element in the casts, the costumes, or the sets, which situates them apart from others. Some theater critics believe, however, that context clues should be taken from the play's text when designing and casting a Shakespearean play. Others disagree in their reviews and contend that techniques and effects of the modern stage could only further enhance Shakespeare's texts. Regardless of modernization, if Shakespeare's language in *Macbeth* is maintained, then aspects of theater (such as the set, the costumes, and the association of an actor with their character or characters) will be easily accepted and enjoyed by more audience members than just the critic or the Shakespearean expert.

Keeping the language intact as much as possible is crucial not only for specific context clues regarding plot, but also may guide directors with clues as to how Shakespeare may have directed *Macbeth* in the Elizabethan era. Therefore, overly modernizing a Shakespearean play with special effects, elaborate set designs, present-day costumes,

Jennifer Bryant is a recent graduate of Frostburg State University, with a major in English Literature and a minor in Theatre. She plans to either attend a Master's program in Literature or in Teaching, so that she can obtain a certificate in order to teach high school English.

and highly amplified music would only encumber a production, according to some reviewers. Yu Jin Ko indirectly acknowledges this aspect in a review where the production was accompanied by overpowering music throughout the entire show at Wellesley College's Ozawa Hall. While the music was enjoyable at first and served as an effective transition between scenes, there was a "distressing impulse to shush the musicians" once the dialogue began (161). This was especially so during Macbeth's soliloquies as the music became more of a "competing, and sometimes irritating, distraction" for the actors to be heard by the audience (Ko 161). During Shakespeare's lifetime, music could not be artificially amplified in the way it would have been with the production seen by Ko. Any natural acoustics offered by Shakespeare's playing space would have given vocalizations an equal chance to be carried along with any music being used. For Shakespearean plays specifically, the "Elizabethan staging method" is the best route to travel as this "freeze[s his] plays in a distant past" (Jones-Hyde 95). Such a stage includes a limited or improvised set, basic yet relatable costumes, and actors who can convincingly play characters as separate beings. On the other hand, in her review of the Clarence Brown Theatre's production, Tara E. Lynn acknowledges that while Shakespeare's language should remain as true to the text as possible, it has the ability to transcend "intricate staging maneuvers ... to guide the audience from point A to point B" (81-82). Lynn's statement implies that directors should not attempt to appeal to Shakespearean experts alone by relying purely on language to convey the plot and the characters' actions. A great many number of novice students attend Shakespearean plays for study and pleasure purposes, and directors should expect them as members of their audiences (Lynn 80). Not only should this include the set, but the costumes should be considered as well.

The visual elements embellishing the actors' play area usually make the first impression on viewers, so an effective set design is crucial to beginning a successful production of *Macbeth*. For Moisés Kaufman's directorial concept, reviewer Michael Basile felt the designers maintained a cohesive set with "bombed and crumbling" military barracks for the production's backdrop (111). This theme of modern war is a popular picture that directors choose for *Macbeth* and, according to reviewers such as Julie Sanders, some design teams are "all too conscious of the looming shadow of the other productions" (102). Whether or not director Rupert Goold was aware of Kaufman's modern-war design, his set designer used war as the theme in a production featuring Patrick Stewart. Instead of a decaying edifice, however, a military operating room that was "dressed bleakly in white tiles and harshly illuminated with industrial lighting" became the visual backdrop (Millard 42). While these two sets may succeed at their visual mastery, some reviewers warn directors a set should never encroach on the playing space and restrict actors. As mentioned previously, the ability possessed by the language to connect with the audience on its own should not be infringed upon, as freezing Shakespeare's plays into his era would be ideal, especially in "an intimate [staging] environment" (Jones-Hyde 95). The Nottingham Playhouse's production chose to ignore these warnings, thus "hemming ... the performance space" to the point where the actors were locked within their own world by a wall that prevented active audience engagement (Sanders 104).

The clothing characters wear is also important and should contribute to a cohesive production aesthetic and, in many productions of *Macbeth*, forgo utilization of an Elizabethan theme. Here, the usage of "simple colors like blue, gray, gold, and beige" on an equally simplistic set would challenge audience members to engage their imaginations and rely upon the language to fill in the missing theatricalities (Jones-Hyde 95). Many modern-day directors, however, go against this idea and apply an updated design to the costumes along with the set. The aforementioned war-themed set designs were accompanied by witches masked in white as in the production reviewed by Sanders (102) and battle fatigues for the soldiers in the production featuring Patrick Stewart (Millard 42). These are obviously not the only available costuming choices, however. In versions of *Macbeth* where actors are double-cast into multiple roles, character specific costumes that do not allow for simple quick-changes would make little sense since costumes assist audiences in associating actors with characters from scene to scene. The prospect of double-casting may be nearly impossible to do in a production with such strong characters, especially when so many appear in several scenes at once. In such scenes, Tara E. Lynn further points out that "the minute changes in costume, such as adding a headband and changing posture, [do] little to alleviate the confusion" between characters (79). On the other hand, poor costume choices are not the only concern when choosing to double-cast actors in a cast of twenty-nine characters.

When double-casting actors for *Macbeth*, directors should limit confusion for audiences as to which actor is playing which character. While costumes may assist in clarifying this dilemma, audiences can have difficulty associating individual actors with their assigned characters regardless. Therefore, Lynn cautions against limiting cast numbers to avoid having actors play multiple characters in a scene (79). Double-casting may also undermine certain characters given to an actor. For example, Sanders notes in her review that Jimmy Chisholm, playing both the Porter and Duncan, could not keep both characters in their distinct high class or low class societal positions (103). Conversely, in the same production, one of the witches also portrayed Fleance and Lady Macduff, which could potentially make the witches "be seen as agents in their muted reappearance in other roles" (Sanders 103). Double-casting may also result in a lessened presence of a character caused by line cuts. As observed in Michael Shurgot's review of director Russ Banham's production, several lines were cut along with several characters to allow for a cast of six actors to portray all twenty-nine roles (98). Unfortunately, this "eviscerated the vitality of several scenes" (98) in a way that removed the need for smaller-speaking and non-speaking roles, leaving the banquet scene, for example, virtually empty of noble attendants. Once again, a return to maintain the integrity of Shakespeare's language is made which indicates line cuts should be avoided. Therefore, limiting cast numbers for a play such as *Macbeth* is impractical.

Like the directors being reviewed, not all critics and reviewers agree on an exact way to formulate and produce an idea or theme for Shakespeare's *Macbeth*. Most do at least acknowledge that conveying the language should come first in order to limit confusion for audience members. After all, language is where directors and designers begin investigating their themes, for the text acts is the primary source. This investigation attempts to first understand the world and the characters driving the action so that boundaries or restrictions become apparent before the larger aspects of designing and construction can begin. Once the text's boundaries and compatible suggestions become apparent, then ideas are free to wander and flow. Among the restrictions and boundaries established by the text, directors should also be aware of the novice Shakespearean's presence in the audience and should limit confusion for them most of all. Only then can an entire audience properly enjoy the casting, setting, and costuming of *Macbeth* through both the spoken and unspoken languages of the theater.

Works Cited

Basile, Michael. "Macbeth." *Shakespeare Bulletin* 24.4 (2006): 109-112.
Jones-Hyde, Rita. "Macbeth." *Shakespeare Bulletin* 25.4 (2007): 95-97.
Ko, Yu Jin. "Shakespeare in New England, 2007." *Shakespeare Bulletin* 26.1 (2008): 161-174.
Lynn, Tara E. "Macbeth." *Shakespeare Bulletin* 26.3 (2008): 77-82.
Millard, Rosie. "Bloody, bold, and resolute." *New Statesman* 137.4865 (2007):
Sanders, Julie. "Review of Shakespeare's *Macbeth* (directed by Lucy Pitman-Wallace) at Nottingham Playhouse, October-November 2008." *Shakespeare* 5.1 (2009): 101-104.
Shurgot, Michael W. "Macbeth." *Shakespeare Bulletin* 25.4 (2007): 98-101.

Who Needs the External World Anyway?: Analyzing the Computational Theory and Methodological Solipsism

Stephanie Amalfe
The Johns Hopkins University

Imagine having the ability to identify an individual's beliefs, thoughts, and convictions simply by looking at a brain scan. No, this is not a science fiction novel or a trailer to an upcoming movie; instead, this view of being able to neurologically see thoughts is one that Jerry Fodor holds. In his 1975 work, *The Language of Thought*, Fodor states that the content of someone's beliefs about, say, a flower has absolutely nothing to do with the plant in the external world (328). Furthermore, Fodor notes that such a flower would not involve any remnant of a commonly accepted societal definition of what a flower is. In essence, everything is determined internally with no interaction with the outside world. How can this view exist? After all, we are flooded with novel stimuli that interact and interweave into new experiences every day. By holding such an extreme position, Fodor is faced to support the position of methodological solipsism ("Methodological Solipsism" 488).

Breaking down the term of methodological solipsism, solipsism is the skeptical view that the external world and other minds cannot be known and might not exist entirely (486). In other words, methodological solipsism postulates the existence of a complete explanatory level dealing exclusively with mental processes within an organism. The

Stephanie Amalfe majors in Cognitive Science at Johns Hopkins University. After graduating in 2011, she will apply to a doctoral program in neuroscience. There she plans a research project on the neurological basis of eating disorders, particularly the relation of the lack of impulse control to binge eating.

most powerful motive for this suggestion is the computational theory of mind, which compares cognitive processing to a computational model. The computational theory states that cognition is a matter of manipulating symbols in accordance with formal algorithms (Turing 440). Consequently, any interpretation that the elements of a computer program may have in the external world is irrelevant to the execution of such program. This computational line of thought has been severely challenged by Daniel Dennett in three focal areas: biographical coherence, finite mental space, and content (*Intentional* 506). In accordance with Dennett's interpretationist criticism, my essay will focus on why the computational theory is committed to methodological solipsism and why such commitment results in an incomplete theory of mind.

Before undertaking Dennett's critical outlook on the computational theory of mind, it is first important to understand that the computational theory denies that any existing computer is, or has, a mind. Rather, it is the claim that having a mind consists of being structurally similar to a computer, or more plausibly, an elaborate assembly of many computers, all which subserve a specific mental capacity (i.e. perception, memory, language processing etc.). Accordingly, all of these computers are united in a complex computational system in which the output of one subsystem serves as the input to another. This system is, therefore, not sensitive to the interpretations assigned to its internal states, but focuses only on the formal symbol it is operating on according to a set of physically determined rules. With these features considered, it is clear that the computational theory has no chance of being a true theory of mind unless the assumption embodied in methodological solipsism is also true. The question, however, arises on how meaning is assigned to a system that remains completely internal. In other words, how can the arbitrary symbols, states, and processes of a computational system be interpreted as meaningful, in light of what is known about an organism's interactions with its environment?

Fodor offers an explanation to the content dilemma through his language of thought hypothesis. According to Fodor, a belief's semantics is dependent on syntax ("Psychosemantics" 67). Syntax refers to the formal rules and principles that govern sentence structure. Semantics refers to a sentence's overall meaning. Fodor claims that mental representations have both syntactic and semantic properties in the same sense that the elements of a natural language do (69). Sentences, for example, differ in shape, just as the words they comprise are different or differently arranged. Each belief is therefore discretely determined by its syntax. As a result, the relationships among mental representations that explain mental processes are the same as the syntactic and semantic relations that obtain among sentences.

Considering Fodor's notion of formally identifying each belief, Dennett offers his first critique towards the computational theory: the issue of finite mental space. In Dennett's article, "Toward a Cognitive Theory of Consciousness," he argues that if every belief was, as Fodor asserts, syntactically distinct, the internal processing system must contain certain components in order to adhere to methodological solipsism (331). The first component would store the individually defined beliefs. The second, an explicator device, would retrieve a particular belief from the storage unit. When considering the idea of a storage unit, however, the concern of generative grammar emerges. The action of defining representations infers that a system's productivity is methodologically limited to the finite vocabulary, defined subsystems, and algorithms that compose it. Such cognitive limitations would be detrimental to a theory of mind. Next, Dennett questions how the storage unit and explicator device would interact with one another. In theory, each component of the computational system is defined by a certain set of algorithms. In this instance, such algorithms not only guide the explicator's actions towards the particular belief in the storage unit, but also suggest the presence of another mechanism to define the actions of the initial explicator device. This solution, therefore, leads to an infinite regress. At this point in his argument, Dennett postulates that the only way to terminate the regress is to assume that there are mental capacities that cannot be linguistically represented by strictly the system itself ("Toward a Cognitive Theory" 337). If his assumption is correct, the computational theory's commitment to methodological solipsism falls short.

Remaining on the topic of computational subdivisions, Dennett is able to offer his second critical stance regarding a belief's content. As explained in the previous paragraph, a mind can mimic a computer in the sense that it can formally and independently link each word of a mental lexicon (syntax) in a specific order to form a certain meaning or intention (semantics). This causal role is based on how the world is represented in our mental states as opposed to how the world actually is. In a sense, natural language is therefore an expression of thought in which computation presupposes representations. Concerning the content of such representations, Dennett claims that if language of thought were possible, there would be no reason why such "brain writing" couldn't be recorded ("Toward a Cognitive Theory" 334). Known as the brain-writing hypothesis, Dennett suggests that the same algorithms identified within a computational system can also be identified neurologically through a language of "neurolese" (336). In other words, if an individual's neural activity were frozen during a particular thought, such as the flower from the previous example, their neuronal firing should identify what they believe. To further conceptualize this idea along the lines of the computational model, imagine that the frozen individual was hooked up to a data printer that displayed a list of the mental sentences that were created. How could one decipher which mental sentence was a belief strictly by reading the data from the printout? With this question in mind, the computational theory must confront the drawbacks of solely determining a belief's meaning through syntax.

Dennett's second critical stance of biographical coherence demonstrates the importance of assigning meaning beyond syntax. Biographical coherence refers to the idea that a belief cannot discretely exist; instead, a belief is interconnected within an individual's whole belief system ("Rediscovery" 163). In order to make Dennett's criticism more clear, suppose there exists a malicious scientist that implants beliefs into people's brains via neurolese. One day, Jane, an only child, gets the belief, "I have a brother in Cleveland," implanted into her brain. Although false, she naively responds, "I have a brother in Cleveland" when later asked about her family. Consequently, Jane becomes confused because the belief, "I have a brother in Cleveland" conflicts with her already existing belief that she is an only child. Simply adding a neurological sentence to the brain therefore doesn't entail that Jane believes the implanted claim. In order for Fodor's mental language stance to hold, the scientist would have to implant numerous beliefs that coincide with the beliefs already present in her mind. In this sense, Jane implicitly commits to logical constancy because her holistic belief, the interconnection of all beliefs, allow for her behavior to be rationalized through normative terms.

Based on Dennett's last argument, it is clear that methodological solipsism restricts the computational theory's ability to offer a rational account of behavior because it lacks a holistic representation of belief. However, when considering a judgment, the computational theory may be able to offer a better explanation for behavior. With this assumption in mind, one must first decipher between a belief and a judgment. A belief is in relation to many other mental states. A judgment is a distinct action. Based on the brain-writing hypothesis, each judgment can therefore be taken without considering the beliefs that it acts upon. Using Dennett's example of Sam the art dealer, Sam could make the judgment that his son is the world's greatest artist. We predict his behavior based on the fact that he constantly praises his son's artwork, even though it is in fact mediocre. However, do our observations imply that Sam truly believes his son is a great artist? Two different belief descriptions can be applied here. Either Sam is in complete denial of his son's mediocrity, or he is aware, but instead acts contrary to his true belief. Both allow for a belief description to be formed, and both descriptions are possible when considered individually. However, if the data printer, hooked up to Sam's mind, reads the neurolese sentence, "I believe my son is a great artist," one would remain clueless as to which belief description Sam utilizes. The idea that two different semantic definitions can result from one physically distinct belief not only strongly opposes Fodor's language of thought, but also solidifies the idea that a sentence's logical form (syntax) does not exclusively attribute a semantic component (content) to a sentence.

Another example will further clarify this flaw in the computational theory. Suppose that Nick is the world's leading philosopher, a renowned ballerina, and Sam's dance teacher. I know nothing of Nick's glorious dance success, but have long admired his work in philosophy. Sam, on the other hand, though blissfully ignorant of Nick's career in philosophy, is in awe of his ability to light up the dance floor. Now, suppose that I am sitting in a café and Nick walks in. I believe that the world's leading philosopher has entered the café. Sam, however, believes that the world's greatest ballet dancer has entered the café. In essence Sam and I are both correct, and what makes us correct is that we both believe that Nick has entered the café. The very same fact, our beliefs about Nick, makes both of the statements true. In fact, if Nick and I were hooked up to the data printer, a scientist would be able to report that both of us believe that Nick has entered the café. However, a problem arises concerning content. On the one hand, if the content of the belief, Nick, is what matters, then we believe the same thing. On the other hand, if the functional role that belief plays in our internal information-processing system is what matters, we do not believe the same thing since my belief is connected with other beliefs about philosophy and Sam's is connected with other beliefs about ballet. In terms of Fodor's language of thought, Sam and I would have different beliefs since our thoughts were physically different. If the mind is considered a computational system, a person's beliefs, being internally classified by pre-programmed representations, raise the original question of how a belief is deemed a belief strictly by being about something. Hence, the computational theory remains an incomplete depiction of mind because it is debarred from raising questions about the semantic properties of mental representations while committing to their existence.

Fodor, in turn, gives few details about how a causal theory is able to remain compatible with methodological solipsism. One would suppose this result to show either that methodological solipsism cannot provide an adequate theory of mind since it cannot account for intentionality (the properties or "aboutness" of a mental state). In addition, one could also suppose that a causal account for intentionality is incorrect since it is incompatible with methodological solipsism. Fodor, however, draws a different response to Dennett's criticism. He claims that because individuals cannot explain their own mental representations, mental representation itself is strictly not a feature of mental states ("Methodological Solipsism" 488). If Fodor is correct, mental representations are not a concern to representational theories of mind in general. As a result, this bizarre notion tremendously weakens the computational theory because mental representation is the foundation on which theories of minds are built.

By being incapable of managing the three key concepts of intentionality, inner independence, and causal relations to the world, the computational theory is flawed. After considering Dennett's critical response, it is clear that methodological solipsism, even at the core of the computational theory, weakens its argument due to its restricting and circular qualities.

Works Cited

Dennett, D. C. "Toward a Cognitive Theory of Consciousness." *Brainstorms: Philosophical Essays on Mind and Psychology*. Cambridge, MA: MIT Press, 1978: 325-338.
Dennett, D. C. *The Intentional Stance*. Cambridge, MA: MIT Press, 1987.
Fodor, J. A. *The Language of Thought*. New York: Crowell, 1975.
———. "Methodological Solipsism Considered as a Research Strategy in Cognitive Psychology." *The Nature of Mind*. D. Rosenthal, ed. Oxford: Oxford University Press, 1990: 485-501.
———. *Psychosemantics*. Cambridge, MA: MIT Press, 1987.

Searle, J. R. *Rediscovery of the Mind*. Cambridge, MA: MIT Press, 1992.
Turing, A. M. "Computing Machinery and Intelligence." *Mind* 59 (1950): 433-460.

Submission guidelines

Proto welcomes scholarly articles and creative non-fiction essays. Submissions can be from current or recent undergraduates; we do not consider papers written for a graduate program. Please use MLA guidelines for quotations and sources. Only one submission per student; essays should be no longer than 5,000 words.

Submissions should be sent either electronically or by U.S. mail to:

Alex Hooke
Professor of Philosophy
Stevenson University
1525 Greenspring Valley Road
Stevenson, MD 21153-0641
ahooke@stevenson.edu

The future of publishing...today!

Apprentice House is the country's only campus-based, student-staffed book publishing company. Directed by professors and industry professionals, it is a nonprofit activity of the Communication Department at Loyola Univeristy Maryland.

Using state-of-the-art technology and an experiential learning model of education, Apprentice House publishes books in untraditional ways. This dual responsibility as publishers and educators creates an unprecedented collaborative environment among faculty and students, while teaching tomorrow's editors, designers, and marketers.

Outside of class, progress on book projects is carried forth by the AH Book Publishing Club, a co-curricular campus organization supported by Loyola University's Office of Student Activities.

Student Project Team for *Proto: An Undergraduate Humanities Journal:*
    Kaitlin Pisano '11

To learn more about Apprentice House books or to obtain submission guidelines, please visit www.ApprenticeHouse.com.

Apprentice House
Communication Department
Loyola University Maryland
4501 N. Charles Street
Baltimore, MD 21210
Ph: 410-617-5265 • Fax: 410-617-2198
info@apprenticehouse.com

www.ingramcontent.com/pod-product-compliance
Lightning Source LLC
Chambersburg PA
CBHW081355040426
42451CB00017B/3460